THE PROMS IN PICTURES

A PICTORIAL HISTORY CELEBRATING THE CENTENARY OF THE PROMS

Edited by George Hall and Matías Tarnopolsky

Text by Andrew Huth

D1081426

Front cover photograph: Godfrey Macdomnic
Back cover photograph: Lou Stone

BBC BOOKS

ALEX VON KOETTLITZ

Published by BBC Books,
an imprint of BBC Worldwide Publishing.
BBC Worldwide Limited, Woodlands,
80 Wood Lane, London W12 0TT

First published 1995
© BBC Concerts Publications 1995

INTRODUCTION

Music, for me, has always been as much about looking as listening; this is why I love going to concerts. There is something fascinating about watching music being made. Even if the performers are static and expressionless, their physical involvement in music-making tells you a great deal about their approach to music. I do not only mean the athleticism of conductors like Barbirolli or Bernstein, jumping about and practically dancing to the music, or even Glenn Gould or Rudolf Serkin chatting away to themselves while they played, but the rapport between the conductor and the orchestral musicians and soloists.

We shall never know how Liszt or Chopin, Berlioz or Wagner looked on the platform – though it is not difficult to imagine from the portraits of them. But from the late nineteenth century onwards music is regularly captured by the camera, and even without movement you can sense something of the musicians' presence.

Perhaps because the Queen's Hall was nearly new when the Proms started, it too was a focus of interest for the photographer, and a surprising number of pictures survive from the early years. This delightful book not only tells the history of the hundred years of the Proms, but sets it in the context of performers and audiences in changing social conditions. What did early Promenaders wear? Why do orchestras still wear the evening dress of a hundred years ago?

Much has changed, but some things remain, and even the early photographs suggest the evolving atmosphere of this extraordinary institution. Whether in the old Queen's Hall, or the vaster spaces of the Royal Albert Hall, there is a palpable mood of concentration and enjoyment.

This book may offer many surprises for the younger concert-goers and will certainly reawaken many happy memories in older music lovers at the point when the Proms move forward into their second century.

Sir John Drummond, CBE
Director, BBC Henry Wood Promenade
Concerts, 1986–95

ALEX VON KOETTLITZ

FOREWORD

Over the last few years a regular feature of the Proms Guide has been an article on some aspect of Proms history – whether items about the Queen's Hall, Sir Henry Wood and other performers from earlier decades, or looking at some of the many works first played at the Proms. In researching these and other articles, the members of the BBC Concerts Publications team have uncovered a wealth of illustrative material relating to the Proms from virtually every period of their existence. The chance to produce a book celebrating one hundred years of the Proms gave us an opportunity to bring a selection of our discoveries together in more permanent form, as well as to research further into what images might exist, helping to bring the early Proms alive for those of us who were not actually there, and to remind others of pleasant musical evenings spent in Kensington or, indeed, Langham Place.

Haydn

But even a picture book should contain more than pictures. For our main text Andrew Huth has written an entertaining and highly informative account of 100 years of the Proms, and we have drawn on the researches of the indefatigable David Harman for our quotations. John Bury, whose original and highly inventive work has given the Proms such a distinctive visual identity over the last nine years, has once again been our designer.

Beethoven

The busts, which once adorned the façade of the Queen's Hall, were rescued from the ruins and are now held in a private collection

The idea for a Proms book began with Charles Shiddell and his colleagues at BBC Audio International, and to him, Jamie Pearson and Mark Barrett we offer thanks for their enthusiastic endorsement of our work at each stage. Equally supportive have been Hans van Woerkens and Arend van Teutem of IMP. Thanks are also due to Chris Weller and Heather Holden-Brown of BBC Books.

Throughout we have relied on the support and encouragement of John Drummond, whose interest and constructive criticism have been invariably useful. His successor, Nicholas Kenyon, has also supported our project from its inception.

In particular we would like to thank the staff and curators of a large number of libraries and archives, as well as various

Promenaders of all ages enjoy an August Bank Holiday programme by the Williams Fairey Engineering Band in Hyde Park in 1988

4

Members of the 1994 Proms team

individuals, for making rare material and their time available to us. These include Nikki Smith of the BBC Picture Library; the staff of the BBC Written Archives Centre at Caversham; Angela Minshull of the Hulton Deutsch Collection; Oliver Davies and Paul Collen of the Royal College of Music; Rosalind Cyphus and Janet Snowman of the Royal Academy of Music; Jacky Cowdrey of the Royal Albert Hall; Richard Mangan of the Mander and Mitchenson Theatre Collection; Vivian Liff of the Stuart-Liff Collection; Paul Nicholls of the Performing Right Society; Peter Joslin; Colin Bradbury; Keith Shelley; Eduardo Bennaroch; Milein Cosman; Georgia Edwards; Lawson Cooke; Dinah Garrett and Norma Gilbert.

For images from recent decades, we have relied heavily on the art of three photographers, Malcolm Crowthers, Alex von Koettlitz and Godfrey Macdomnic. Their outstanding skills in capturing musical performances in visual terms provide much of the material for the later chapters.

In addition, every member of the Proms team has contributed, directly or indirectly, to the contents of this book, and in particular we would like to thank Stephen Maddock, Nicola Goold, Ann Richards and Liz Russell; and both the full-time and itinerant members of BBC Concerts Publications, especially Karen Cardy, Jenny Slater, Jan Hart and Katina Dawe, and once again David Harman, this time for his proof-reading.

Bach

In spite of the latter, any mistakes or omissions are entirely the responsibility of the editors. Inevitably, there are certain areas we have covered less fully than we might have wished, and for any omissions and mistakes, and to anyone we have neglected to thank, we make our apologies in advance.

George Hall and Matías Tarnopolsky
Henry Wood House, above the site of the Queen's Hall

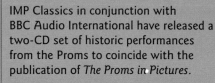

IMP Classics in conjunction with BBC Audio International have released a two-CD set of historic performances from the Proms to coincide with the publication of *The Proms in Pictures*.

Berlioz
Grande Symphonie Funèbre et Triomphale. Final movement: Apothéose
Sir John Pritchard, BBC SO, 1983

Tchaikovsky
Nutcracker Suite
Sir Malcolm Sargent, BBC SO, 1966

Elgar
Symphony No. 1
Sir Adrian Boult, BBC SO, 1976

Gluck
'Che disse? ch'ascoltai?', 'Addio, addio, o miei sospiri' from *Orfeo ed Euridice*.
Dame Janet Baker (Orfeo),
Raymond Leppard,
London Philharmonic Orchestra, 1982

Wagner
Overture and Venusberg Music from *Tannhäuser*
Sir Thomas Beecham,
Royal Philharmonic Orchestra, 1954

Strauss
Suite *Der Rosenkavalier*
Sir John Barbirolli,
Hallé Orchestra, 1969

Janáček
Sinfonietta
Rudolf Kempe, BBC SO, 1974

Vincent Youmans arr. Shostakovich
Tea for Two ('Tahiti Trot')
Gennady Rozhdestvensky, BBC SO, 1981

These records will be available on their own, or as part of a Proms Centenary Presentation box, containing the discs, the present volume and a third CD consisting of speeches from the Last Night of the Proms by Sir Henry Wood, Sir Malcolm Sargent, Sir Colin Davis, Sir John Pritchard, Mark Elder, Normal Del Mar, James Loughran and Andrew Davis, introduced by the Director of the BBC Proms, John Drummond CBE.

· QUEEN'S HALL, W. ·

Lessee and Manager - ROBERT NEWMAN.

PROMENADE CONCERTS

SEASON 1895

(UNDER THE DIRECTION OF MR. ROBERT NEWMAN).

Programme for this Evening, Saturday, August 10th, 1895, at Eight o'clock.

DOORS OPEN AT 7 O'CLOCK EVERY EVENING.

MADAME MARIE DUMA.	MRS. VAN DER VEER-GREEN.
MR. IVER McKAY.	
MR. FFRANGCON-DAVIES.	MR. W. A. PETERKIN.

Flute - MR. A. FRANSELLA.
Bassoon - MR. E. F. JAMES.
Cornet - MR. HOWARD REYNOLDS.

FULL ORCHESTRA. Leader - - MR. W. FRYE PARKER.

ACCOMPANIST - MR. H. LANE WILSON.

Conductor = MR. HENRY J. WOOD.

PROMENADE OR BALCONY - ONE SHILLING.

SEASON TICKETS (Transferable) ONE GUINEA. GRAND CIRCLE SEATS (Numbered and Reserved) 2/6.

No Charge for Booking Seats. Seats Reserved the whole Evening.

FLORAL DECORATIONS BY MESSRS. WILLS & SEGAR, ONSLOW CRESCENT, SOUTH KENSINGTON.

Theodore Nicholl, ✍

ONLY AT

306, High Holborn.

Directly opposite First Avenue Hotel.

SPÉCIALITÉ-
EVENING DRESS.

**HIGH-CLASS
TAILORING**

AT

Moderate Charges.

THE SUIT (lined throughout silk) from £5.

SPATEN-BEER.

GABRIEL SEDLMAYR,
BRAUEREI ZUM SPATEN (MUNICH).
London Depot: 107, CHARING CROSS ROAD, W.C.

TO BE HAD AT THE BARS.
Supplied in Perfect Condition in Casks and Bottles from the above address.
P.S.— Ask your Grocer for it.

For Advertisements on these Programmes application should be made to

CHARLES DEWYNTER, Limited.

Agents and Contractors for Advertisements,

23, HAYMARKET, LONDON, S.W.

Price Twopence.

Right: *Programme for the very first of Robert Newman's Queen's Hall Promenade Concerts, 10 August 1895*

Below: *Sketch for proposed concert hall at Langham Place,* The Builder, *14 February 1891*

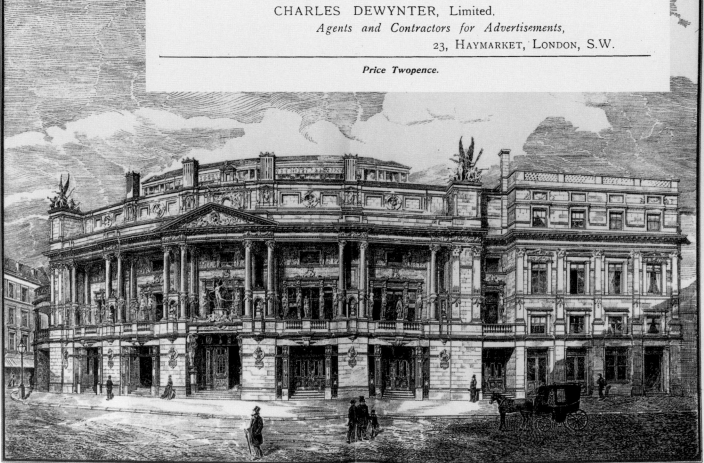

PROPOSED CONCERT HALL, LANGHAM PLACE.—Mr. T. E. KNIGHTLEY, F.R.I.B.A., ARCHITECT.
EXTERIOR VIEW

10 AUGUST 1895

Eight o'clock on Saturday evening, 10 August 1895. Mr Henry J. Wood, with a long white baton in his hand and a carnation in his buttonhole, takes up his position on the rostrum of the Queen's Hall in Langham Place. He conducts the newly-formed orchestra in the National Anthem, then launches into Wagner's *Rienzi* Overture. The concert that follows is a curious mixture, designed to thrill, amuse and entertain. There are twenty-five items altogether: popular orchestral favourites, operatic excerpts, solo turns for flute, cornet and bassoon, songs and ballads with piano accompaniment, and so on. The audience, many of whose members are standing in the arena of the hall, loves it. This is just as well, for a great deal of money and thought has gone into this concert, intended as the first of a new summer concert series.

Nobody present that evening, however, least of all Henry Wood, could have imagined just how successful and durable a venture it was to become. This first eight-week season of Promenade Concerts marked the beginning of what was to develop and grow over the years into the world's most remarkable summer music festival – eventually to be known as the Henry Wood Promenade Concerts.

In the course of a century, the Proms have provided a platform for countless great composers and performers, and have introduced many thousands of people to great music, either in the Queen's Hall, the Royal Albert Hall, or through broadcasts. They are now a permanent and irreplaceable feature of the summer months in London, internationally famous and internationally admired.

The young conductor Henry Wood with an 'artistic' cravat

Drawing by Thomas Downey of an 1895 Queen's Hall Prom

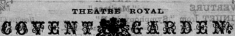

Programmes for nineteenth-century Proms held in various London venues

Jules Prudence Rivière (1819–1900), conductor of popular Promenade Concerts

The entrance to Vauxhall Gardens, early nineteenth century

BACKGROUND

The behind-the-scenes beginnings of the Proms in fact go back much further than that August evening in 1895. The idea of informal concerts where audiences could be increased and prices kept low by the simple expedient of removing much of the seating from the hall was by no means new at the end of the nineteenth century. Such concerts were part of a tradition that went back at least as far as London's famous eighteenth-century pleasure gardens, where 'promenade' really did mean walking around rather than just standing. The pleasure gardens' season lasted from late spring to early autumn, and elaborate concerts, mixing instrumental and vocal music, were an important part of each evening's entertainment. The weather, of course, was an essential factor in the promoters' risk.

The pleasure gardens declined in the early nineteenth century, partly as a result of the increasing industrialisation of London, partly because the all-powerful middle-classes began to feel (probably correctly) that they were not really very respectable. The type of varied musical performance they provided, however, continued in a number of other ways. Many series of light Promenade Concerts took place in the middle years of the nineteenth century in London's music-halls and theatres, such as the Lyceum, the Prince's and Covent Garden. What they all had in common, apart from the mobility of the 'promenade', was a popular choice of music, low prices and – not the least of their attractions – the availability of refreshments.

The most memorable of mid-century Promenade Concerts were those given in the 1840s and 1850s at Drury Lane

Conductor Louis Jullien (1812–60) who ensured 'amusement as well as attempting instruction, by blending in the programmes the most sublime works with those of a lighter school'

A concert at Vauxhall Gardens in 1785, by Thomas Rowlandson (1756–1827)

Covent Garden Theatre. This, the second theatre on the site, was designed by Robert Smirke, opened in 1809 and burned down in 1856

CONDUCTOR,
Mons. MUSARD.
Solo Performers:
NADAUD. Mons. DANTONET. Mons. PROSPERE. Mons. PILET,
DE LOFFRE. Herr MULLER. Herr MULLER. Jun. Mons. PAIVRE,
WILLENT-BORDOGNI. Mons. BARRET. Mons. COLLINET,
Herr KOENIG. Herr FRISCH. Mr. CASE. Mr. HOWELL. Mr. HILL,
Mr. HANCOCK. Mr. JARRETT. Master TAYLOR. Mr. LAZARUS,
And Mr. ELIASON.

Music cover showing a Promenade Concert at Covent Garden Theatre, 1876

PROMENADE QUADRILLE.

**PERFORMED AT THE PROMENADE CONCERTS,
COVENT GARDEN THEATRE.**

CHARLES COOTE JUNR.

INTRODUCING THE POPULAR MELODIES.

"NEVER GIVE IN," "THE SILVERY MOON IS BEAMING," "HOOP LA," "LIFE IS LIKE AN APRIL DAY,"
"TOMMY MAKE ROOM FOR YOUR UNCLE," "DRIVING IN THE PARK," "THEY ALL HAVE A MATE BUT ME,"
"WAIT TILL THE MOONLIGHT," "MULLIGAN GUARDS," "GOLD, GOLD, GOLD," "PULL YOURSELVES TOGETHER."

Ground Plan of Queen's Hall, as envisaged by The Builder in 1891

Proposed Concert Hall, Langham-place.—Plan on Street Level.

in streets. He referred to many wonderful mechanical contrivances, some of which had been tried and condemned, others were being experimented with or were about to be tested as street motors. He thought that the cable system has given by far the best results mechanically and financially. He referred to what had been done abroad and in this country, and explained that the satisfactory results of

Illustrations.

PROPOSED NEW CONCERT HALL, LANGHAM-PLACE.

E give a view of the exterior and interior of this building, which is, we by the colourful French conductor Louis Jullien, who aimed 'to ensure amusement as well as attempting instruction, by blending in the programmes the most sublime works with those of a lighter school'. Jullien's own Quadrilles would appear side by side with music by Mozart, Mendelssohn and Beethoven (to emphasise the sublimity of the latter, Jullien affected white gloves and a jewelled baton).

Throughout the nineteenth century the demand for good music was constantly increasing, and by the 1890s, it was clear that London's musical institutions had not really caught up with this demand. The population of Greater London had more than doubled in the past half-century, and the capital badly needed a new concert hall. At this time the most important existing halls were the Crystal Palace, moved from Hyde Park to Sydenham after the Great Exhibition of 1851, and the St James's Hall in Piccadilly, built in 1858. Concerts at the Crystal Palace were cheap, but it was not easy of access; the St James's Hall was more expensive and more exclusive. The Royal Albert Hall was considered suitable only for large-scale oratorio performances.

In 1891 work started on a new concert hall in Langham Place, near the present-day Broadcasting House. Based vaguely on the Pantheon in Rome, it was intended to be called either Victoria Hall or Queen's Hall. It opened under the latter name in 1893, decorated in shades of red and brown that perfectly reflected the tastes of the age. The main hall had a capacity of nearly 2,500, and in addition there was a small hall suitable for solo recitals and chamber music with a capacity of about 500. Sight lines were good, and everybody agreed that the acoustics were excellent for all types of music. The Queen's Hall was to be the centre of London's musical life for nearly half a century.

Ticket for a Promenade Concert at Covent Garden, 10 August 1881

Programme for Promenade Concert at Her Majesty's Theatre, 19 October 1889

Programme cover for the 1881 season at Covent Garden

Advertisement for
a Wagner Night in
Radio Times, by
Mabel Lapthorn,
1930

WAGNER NIGHT
AT THE QUEEN'S HALL
A PROMENADE CONCERT

relayed from The Queen's Hall, London
(Sole Lessees, Me

TONIG
MARGARET
ARTHU
THE B.B.C. SY
(Leader, C
Conductor,

ORCHESTRA
Introduction, Act III, 'Lohen
Forest Murmurs, 'Siegfried '
Prelude, Act III, 'Tristan and
Cor Anglais, Terrance M

MARGARET BALFOUR
Adriano's Aria, ' Gerechter G

ORCHESTRA
Siegfried's Journey to the Rhi

ARTHUR FEAR
Aria, ' The Term is past,' 'Th

ORCHESTRA
A ' Faust ' Overture
Venusberg Music, ' Tannhäus

On Monday nights you're apt to find the Queen's Hall pretty full,
For Monday night is Wagner night, and Wagner's still a 'pull'.
An amazing chap was Wagner, a by no means such-and-such man,
And it isn't fair to judge him by his early 'Flying Dutchman'.
You should hear young Walther's Prize Song (how his brain the fellow ransacks!),
The Procession of the Masters, and the Monologues of Hans Sachs;
Hear the Prelude to Act III of 'Lohengrin' if you've a mind to;
Forest Murmurs; Siegmund's love-song; Siegfried's journey to the Rhine too.
The forging song of Siegfried is most surely worth a hearing
So is Lohengrin's Narration and the tale of Wotan's spearing.
Other things to be included in this real Wagnerian salad
Are the Overture 'Tannhäuser', Liza's prayer and Senta's ballad;
And if you don't agree with me that Wagner was a wonder,
Either you are much mistaken or the world has made a blunder.

from Diogenes's Handy Guide to the Proms (1939 Edition),
quoted in Robert Elkin, Queen's Hall 1893–1941 [1944]

Proposed design for the interior of Queen's Hall,
The Builder, 14 February 1891

Left: *Exterior of the Queen's Hall*

MANAGER AND CONDUCTOR

Robert Newman

The manager of the new hall was Robert Newman (1858–1926), a man of enterprise and taste with a fine Victorian sense of mission. Long before the days of public subsidy, he was adept at balancing the conflicting claims of art and commerce. He organised regular symphony concerts in the Queen's Hall, but believed that it was also necessary to attract new listeners with more popular programmes. To run these, he needed an orchestra and a conductor. He decided to sound out the young Henry Wood.

Wood, born in London in 1869, had undergone a thorough, traditional musical training, and since his late teens had steadily been making a name for himself as organist, accompanist, vocal coach and conductor of choirs, orchestras and ramshackle opera companies which demanded steady nerves and huge reserves of tact. To this solid musical background he added a capacity for immensely hard work.

Among Wood's great qualities was his utter reliability. He never conducted from memory, feeling that the members of the orchestra would play with more confidence if he had the score in front of him. His wide, firm beat conveyed his musical intentions clearly and precisely, and he knew perfectly what an orchestra could or could not do. A demon for punctuality, he never wasted time, and never allowed anyone else to waste it either. In short, a man after Newman's own heart.

One morning in the spring of 1894 Newman took Wood to look around his new hall. The arena had been cleared of seats. Many years later Wood recalled the scene in his memoirs:

Newman had a brisk, business-like manner and never wasted words. We stood looking down into the arena with its brownish carpet that blended with the dull-fawnish colour of the walls. [...]

"What do you think of the idea of having Promenade concerts here?" asked Newman suddenly.

"Well, with your knowledge of concerts, and given the right orchestra and artists, it should be a grand success."

168 *THE SPHERE* [August 25, 1906]

THE BEGINNING OF THE POPULAR MUSICAL SEASON.

THE ORIGINAL QUEEN'S HALL ORCHESTRA REHEARSING FOR THE PROMENADE CONCERTS

The week begins with Wagner's frenzy:
Perchance the Overture 'Rienzi'.
Anon we trace the subtle line
Of Siegfried's Journey to the Rhine;
Some tenor earns a great ovation
For singing Lohengrin's Narration.

from 'Diogenes the Younger',
Guide to the Proms, Musical Opinion
(1929)

Queen's Hall, 1895–6: the busts of composers
(see pages 4–5) can be clearly seen facing out into
Langham Place

Every young British composer at his first encounter with Sir Henry [Wood] must inevitably be charmed by the latter's ever-ready sympathy and encouragement. [...] My own earliest meeting with him happened in September 1910. He had invited me to send in a work for performance at one of the Proms [the tone-poem In the Faery Hills], and a day or two before the date of the concert summoned me to his house for a preliminary run through on the piano. In youthful trepidation I knocked at his door in Hampstead, wondering what kind of reception I should get from that – even so long ago – almost legendary figure. Almost immediately he hurried into the room and I discovered to my relief that in stature he was actually no more than life-size. Like Elgar, Sir Henry at the rostrum always appeared, by sheer force of personality, to be very much taller than he actually is. [...] His handshake was firm and genial, and in two seconds my nervousness vanished. Getting to work at once (for as ever there was no spare time to waste), he proved kindness itself, showing the keenest interest in and paying the closest attention to my score. At the concert he gave a beautifully balanced rendering of a piece which was at that time considered dangerously modern and uncomfortably difficult to play.

Arnold Bax, 'He is a national institution', in Sir Henry Wood: Fifty Years of the Proms,
ed. Ralph Hill and C. B. Rees [1944]

"Right! Come over to Pagani's and have lunch. We can talk about it there."

I was greatly impressed with Newman over that lunch. I had never met a manager who knew anything about music. Newman did. He possessed both business acumen and artistic ideals. *He wanted the public to come to love great music.*

"I am going to run nightly concerts and train the public by easy stages," he said. "Popular at first, gradually raising the standard until I have *created* a public for classical and modern music." […]

I did not meet him again until he called on me in February, 1895. With hardly a word of greeting he tackled the question of what was obviously uppermost in his mind.

"I have decided to run those Promenade concerts I told you about last year. I want you to be the conductor of a permanent Queen's Hall Orchestra. We'll run a ten weeks' season."

I can still feel the thrill of that moment. An orchestra … in Queen's Hall … My orchestra …

Wood on the podium of the Queen's Hall, 1902, as seen in The Tatler

Wood and Newman made a fine team. If Robert Newman's brisk, military bearing gave him a strong physical resemblance to Lord Kitchener, Wood in his earlier years affected a more 'artistic' appearance, with a rich beard and flowing cravat. ('Are you sure you are *quite* English, Mr Wood?', Queen Victoria asked him after a command performance at Windsor in 1898. Wood's mother was in fact Welsh.)

Newman had the imagination to realise Henry Wood's potential, but initially lacked the money to support the orchestra he needed. He asked Wood if he would be prepared to put up 'some two or three thousand pounds of capital' (a huge sum in those days). Wood had no such sum, but the money was eventually provided by Dr George Cathcart, a wealthy amateur who was a friend of one of Wood's singing pupils. Cathcart made only two stipulations: that Wood should be the sole conductor of the orchestra (he admired above all Wood's conducting of Wagner), and that 'French pitch' – easier for singers, because it was slightly lower than the pitch that had become customary in England – should be adopted. The placing of a fountain in the arena of the hall (a feature later to be carried over to the Royal Albert Hall) also appears to have been Cathcart's idea.

The fountain in the Arena of the Royal Albert Hall, a vestige of Dr Cathcart's influence

QUEEN'S HALL,

W.

Lessee and Manager - - ROBERT NEWMAN.

MR. ROBERT NEWMAN'S

Promenade

SIXTH SEASON, 1900.

UNDER THE DIRECTION OF MR. ROBERT NEWMAN.

EVERY EVENING FROM 8 till 11.
DOORS OPEN AT 7.30.

Concerts

Programme for Saturday, November 3rd, 1900.

Miss **FLORENCE SCHMIDT**
Miss **JESSIE GOLDSACK**
Mr. **D. FFRANGCON-DAVIES**
Mr. **W. H. SQUIRE** - - - Solo Violoncello

ROBERT NEWMAN'S QUEEN'S HALL ORCHESTRA.

PRINCIPAL VIOLIN - - - Mr. **ARTHUR W. PAYNE.**
ORGANIST AND ACCOMPANIST - - Mr. **PERCY PITT.**

Conductor = Mr. HENRY J. WOOD.

PROMENADE - - .ONE

SEASON TICKETS (11 weeks), Trans
BALCONY, 2/- GRAND CIRCLE, Numbered and
SMOKING PERMITTED (except in the portion of Grand Circ

Telephone, 5216, Gerrard.
Telegrams, "Chord, London."

Tickets for all Concerts and Theatres may be obtaine

Boosey & Co.'s Popular Songs

WHEN THE BOYS COME HOME, D, E flat, and G.
F. Allitsen.
EVER SO FAR AWAY, B flat, C, D, and E flat.
Stephen Adams.
A DOLLY AND A COACH, E flat, F, and G.
G. H. Stone.
WHO CARRIES THE GUN? F and G.
Alicia A. Needham.
I WILL GIVE YOU REST, C, D flat, E flat, & F.
THERE'S A LAND D, E flat, F, & G F. H. Cowen.
Allitsen.
Price 2/- net.
BOOSEY & Co., 295 Regent Street, London

YSAYE
CONCERT

(Under the Management of Mr. Robert Newm

November 14th, at 8
November 19th, at 8
November 21st, at 3

TWO ORCHESTRAL CO
will Conduct for
ROBERT NEWMAN'S
of 1

VIOLIN RECITAL by N

Tickets—10/6, 7/6, 5/- (Reserved) ; 2/6, 1/

MR. ROBERT
NEWMAN'S CONCERTS,
QUEEN'S HALL.

Promenade Concerts
Every Evening at 8.

Symphony Concerts.
Full particulars on back page.

The Sunday Concert Society's
Sunday Afternoon Concerts
Every Sunday Afternoon at 3.30.

Chevalier Recitals
Every Afternoon at 3.
Also Thursdays & Saturdays at 8.30.

Ysaye Concerts
Nov. 14th at 8. Orchestral.
Nov. 19th at 8. Orchestral.
Nov. 21st at 3. Violin Recital.

Busoni Pianoforte Recital,
Nov. 27th, at 3.

IND

Queen's Hall, c1910

INTERVAL OF FIFTEEN MINUTES,
DURING WHICH
THE POLYTECHNIC ANIMATED PHOTOGRAPHS will be shown
in the SMALL HALL. Admission Sixpence. This evening's series will be
selected from the following subjects, reproduced with all the actual movements of
real life :—

1. Razing a factory chimney (height, 150 feet) which stood for 80 years at Hooley Bridge, Heywood, and was successfully felled by Mr. T. Smith, the Lancashire steeple-jack, on July 14th, 1900.
2. Tommy's washing day—a scene at Modder River Camp.
3. The Seaforth Highlanders crossing the Modder over a temporary railway bridge erected, in place of one blown up by the Boers, by the Royal Engineers in record time of 40 hours.
4. A skirmish with the Boers near Kimberley by a party of Gen. French's cavalry scouts.
5. A panorama taken from an armoured train.
6. Clearing the bush—giving some idea of the work done by the pioneers. Col. Hope and staff are seen galloping over the newly made roadway.
7. A 5in. siege gun in action at the battle of Pretoria, June 4th, 1900.
8. The Essex Regiment crossing the Vaal River in a waggon punt.
9. The C.I.V.'s March on Johannesburg Showing this gallant Regiment (which has cut a most prominent figure in the capture of Johannesburg) leaving Kroonstadt for the march across the Veldt.
10. The Cameron Highlanders entering Bloemfontein.
11. The surrender of Kroonstaad to Lord Roberts, May 12th, 1900.
12. Canadians crossing the Orange River on pontoon bridge.
13. Mackenzie traction engine drawing war supplies off to the front.
14. Her Majesty entering Dublin.

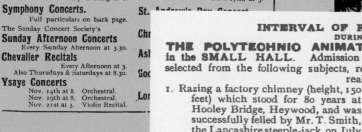

The Polytechnic Animated Photographs were a popular interval feature in the early years. This 1900 sequence included scenes from the Boer War

THE FIRST QUEEN'S HALL PROMS

The name 'Henry Wood Promenade Concerts' was still half a century in the future. At the beginning they were 'Mr Robert Newman's Promenade Concerts', and Mr Henry J. Wood conducted 'Mr Robert Newman's Queen's Hall Orchestra' (the J stood for Joseph).

When Wood dictated his memoirs in the late 1930s, he looked back to the first days of the Proms with a mixture of justifiable pride and amusement. Remembering the very first Queen's Hall Prom, he commented: 'How many of my young Promenaders could stand and listen to it if I repeated it nowadays I leave to their judgment. I doubt whether I could tolerate it myself, but both they and I must remember the conditions ruling then. This was a new venture, and as such it had to be popular'.

However odd some of these early concerts may seem to us today, they achieved just what Wood and Newman intended: they really were popular, and thus created an audience for music. The great variety of the programmes contained possibilities for development in several directions.

The early audiences were not on the whole drawn from fashionable society. One did not have to dress up for the Proms, and nor did one have to save up: a Promenade ticket cost a shilling (5p) for each concert, or a guinea (£1.05) for a season ticket. If symphony concerts in those days could sometimes be rather serious affairs, the Proms deliberately aimed at an informal atmosphere, which must have been reinforced by the eating, drinking and smoking that accompanied the music (although patrons were asked to observe silence during the vocal numbers). Gentlemen were asked to refrain from striking matches while the music was playing (in those days ladies were not expected to smoke at all, and certainly not in public). Rows E and F in the gallery were set aside for non-smokers.

The concerts were planned to last for about three hours, beginning at 8 o'clock and finishing at 11. There were always a large number of items, most of them quite short. The printed programmes pointed out, however, that 'the persistent demands for encores sometimes necessitate the omission of certain items in order to finish within reasonable time'.

Anything that we would now recognise as 'serious' music was

The singer Jessie Goldsack, who made thirty-four appearances at the Proms between 1900 and 1908, singing popular arias and ballads. Later, as Sir Henry's partner, she adopted the name 'Lady Jessie Wood'

The type of audience was different from what it is today. There were comparatively few women – in the Promenade, at all events; not so many adolescents; a fair sprinkling of foreigners, some with flowing locks, floppy ties, loose clothes, and scores under their arms. The enthusiasm was there, but more restrained and judicious – none of the mass hysteria of recent years, which applauds everything indiscriminately; some unfamiliar items in those days got only perfunctory applause. [...]

There was always plenty of room in the Hall in those early days – you could walk about a little without annoying people or getting unduly in their way. [...] Many people habitually listened in the corridor, sitting on the hot-water pipes (which were not very hot). You could also get refreshments at any time during the concert in the refreshment rooms on the Promenade level, under the entrance to the Hall.

J. P. O'Callaghan, who had been present at the first Prom (10 August 1895) quoted in Robert Elkin's Queen's Hall 1893–1941 [1944]

For me, and for thousands like me, the Proms came to serve as a sort of club. One went with a group of friends and patrolled the promenade during the intervals looking out for other friends. After the concert one went off in a group to have coffee. The motif here was, no doubt, largely social. You went, especially if you were a girl – and the Proms were full of pretty girls; or is it that even plain ones look pretty when they are listening to music? – to see and to be seen; but out of every score who began to come out of 'mateyness', one continued to come for the music. Perhaps the percentage was higher than that. Here were hundreds of young people who did not know a crotchet from a quaver coming to the Proms to get a little culture and to see their friends. For one in a dozen, let us say, the music stuck and a new window upon beauty had opened to illuminate their lives. It was Sir Henry [Wood]'s triumph that it was to the Proms that one did go to meet one's friends, and not to the boxing ring, or the dogs, or the dirt track, or in those early days, to the music hall. Had it not been for him, in that one out of twenty – or should it be one out of twelve? – the window would never have opened.

C. E. M. Joad, 'Queen's Hall was my club', in Sir Henry Wood: Fifty Years of the Proms, ed. Ralph Hill and C. B. Rees [1944]

The Russian soprano Olga Mikhailov, Henry Wood's first wife, who made forty-one appearances at the Proms between 1901 and 1909 as Mrs Henry Wood. Her wide repertoire included arias and songs by Tchaikovsky and Rakhmaninov, and the British premiere of Mahler's Fourth Symphony

confined to the first part of the concert. From the second season, members of the audience could pay an extra sixpence (2½p) and spend the fifteen-minute interval in the Small Hall admiring the latest 'Polytechnic Animated Photographs' – among London's earliest film shows. The repertory in 1896 included 'A Peep at Paris', 'Rough Sea, Cornish Coast', 'David Devant, conjuring with Rabbits', 'Factory Gates at Dinner-time' and 'The Coronation of the Czar at Moscow'. A few years later, there would be carefully selected scenes from the Boer War in South Africa.

Charles Santley, the leading baritone of the Victorian era, who performed on five occasions at the Proms between 1896 and 1898, singing arias by Mozart and Gounod, and regularly including his warhorse 'Simon the Cellarer'

The second part of the programme was generally much shorter than the first, and consisted almost entirely of light items. A great attraction was always the Grand Fantasia – choice morsels from popular operas, with instrumental soloists taking the vocal lines. The very first Prom contained a 'Grand Selection' from *Carmen*. Five years later, a single week's Proms featured Grand Fantasias on *Carmen*, *Lohengrin*, *Aida*, *Cavalleria rusticana* (twice), Gounod's *Queen of Sheba* and *Faust*, and Vincent Wallace's *Maritana*.

In the 1890s up to half of a programme might consist of solo items: there were star turns for all sorts of instruments, frequently the cornet, and many songs with piano accompaniment (often ballads of the most rip-roaring patriotism or mawkish sentimentality). These offered a platform for many of the period's notable singers. There were appearances by the veteran Charles Santley, and by Fanny Moody and Charles Manners, the husband-and-wife team who established an opera company bearing their names in 1897. Among the five singers taking part in the very first Prom was David Ffrangcon-Davies, who went on to give fifty-three performances over the next decade.

The noted mezzo-soprano Louise Kirkby Lunn, who made seventy-nine appearances at the Proms between 1895 and 1902. She brought mementos of her Delilah, Carmen and Orpheus to the Proms

Baritone David Ffrangcon-Davies, who appeared at the very first Prom and performed a total of fifty-three times between 1895 and 1906 in a wide variety of operatic excerpts and songs

From Wood's point of view these solo items were useful in not requiring precious orchestral rehearsal time, although Wood himself often spent the hours between morning rehearsal and evening concert coaching the soloists.

The earliest Proms invariably finished with a rousing march or waltz for the full orchestra to send the audiences away happy and – it was hoped – ready for more the following evening.

Insert from the programme of 15 September 1900

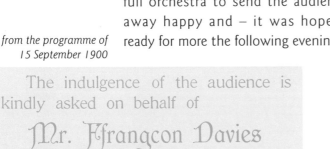

The indulgence of the audience is kindly asked on behalf of

Mr. Ffrangcon Davies

who is suffering from a severe cold.

Charles Manners

Fanny Moody, who made eight appearances between 1896 and 1899, all with her husband Charles Manners. Operas by British composers featured largely in their repertoire. Together they ran and starred with the Moody-Manners Company, which toured Britain from 1898 to 1916

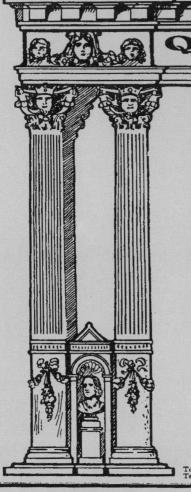

QUEEN'S HALL

Sole Lessees   Messrs. CHAPPELL & Co. Ltd.

THE QUEEN'S HALL ORCHESTRA, Ltd.

Directors—

SIR EDGAR SPEYER, BART., *Chairman.*

THE EARL HOWE, G.C.V.O.   H. EGAN HILL, ESQ.
LT.-COL. ARTHUR COLLINS, C.B.   HENRY J. WOOD, ESQ.
Secretary -   F. POPE.

PROMENADE CONCERTS

AUGUST 17th to OCTOBER 26th, 1907.

Every Evening at 8.   Doors open at 7.30.

THURSDAY, AUG. 22nd, 1907, at 8.

Miss MAUD SANTLEY.

Mr. JULIEN HENRY.

Solo Pianoforte—

Mr. CLAUDE GASCOIGNE.

THE QUEEN'S HALL ORCHESTRA

Principal Violin   -   Mr. H. VERBRUGGHEN.
Organist & Accompanist   Mr. FREDK. B. KIDDLE.

Conductor   -   -   Mr. HENRY J. WOOD.

Promenade, 1/-; Balcony, 2/-; Grand Circle (numbered and reserved), 3/- & 5/-. Season Tickets (Transferable), available till October 25th—Promenade, 21/-.

Smoking Permitted (except in the portion of Grand Circle reserved for non-smokers).

The QUEEN'S HALL ORCHESTRA, Ltd., 320 Regent Street, W.

Telephone—551 Paddington.
Telegrams—"Accompany, London."   ROBERT NEWMAN, Manager.

PRICE TWOPENCE.

'TRAINING THE PUBLIC IN EASY STAGES...'

These early programmes seem now to be an extraordinary mixture of the acceptably serious, the acceptably light, and the downright trivial. All the time, though, Wood and Newman were succeeding in their aim of raising standards and introducing the Prom audiences to a wider and more serious range of music. The thirtieth concert of the very first season was a Beethoven Night which included the *Egmont* Overture, the Fifth Piano Concerto and the Fifth Symphony. As early as the second Proms season in 1896, the tradition was established of Wagner Night on Monday and Beethoven Night on Friday – a tradition that would continue for several decades. Within a very few years, the ballads and the cornet solos had begun to fade away, and improbable fantasias on operatic tunes were giving way to properly prepared extracts from the operas.

By the 1900 season all nine of Beethoven's symphonies were being regularly played (although the Ninth generally lacked its choral finale). A 1902 Prom contained both the First Piano Concerto and First Symphony by Brahms – a combination that would have been considered impossibly 'serious' seven years earlier.

By the turn of the century Wood had introduced a great deal of music by such 'modern' composers as Rimsky-Korsakov, Richard Strauss, Tchaikovsky, Chabrier, Glazunov, Dvořák, Saint-Saëns and Balakirev. Wood's enthusiasm for Russian music was stimulated by his Russian

Henry Wood

PRIVATE COLLECTION

MISS SUSAN STRONG.

Present-day Promenaders will be interested to know that the first appearance of their favourite Myra Hess at these concerts [...] belongs to this season of 1908 when she played Liszt's E flat concerto – not the type of music with which she is generally associated in these days. Curiously enough, I was rather long in securing her for a Promenade. Not that Robert Newman was disinterested – quite on the contrary, he knew that she had made an impression the previous year with a Beethoven concerto in a concert of her own at Queen's Hall. It just happened that we had been inundated with pianists; there was nothing more in it that that. However, once Newman did engage Miss Hess, he re-engaged her as many as five or six times in a single season. Myra Hess has never lost the fascination she exerted over her audience then. She is perhaps best known for her rich, romantic interpretation of the Schumann concerto but she displays no less musical style – which is often intense – when she plays the Brahms concerto in B flat. She still seems to me the dark-haired girl she was in 1908. She is more fortunate than a good many of us in that she has changed very little in appearance with the years. Her musicianship has matured – whose does not in thirty years? – but she was the great artist, even then.

Henry J. Wood, My Life of Music (1938)

Percy Grainger (1883–1961) (left) with the Hollywood star Ramon Navarro. Grainger made seven appearances at the Proms between 1904 and 1948, including the British premiere of Tchaikovsky's First Piano Concerto on 17 August 1904. His first work to be heard at the Proms was Mock Morris in 1912. He made a notable posthumous appearance on the 1988 Last Night, when his piano roll recording of Grieg's Piano Concerto was accompanied by Andrew Davis and the BBC Symphony Orchestra

Left, centre: A much-loved figure in British musical life, Myra Hess made ninety-two appearances stretching over fifty-three years (1908-61). These included concertos by Beethoven on thirty-two occasions, by Bach on fifteen, and the Schumann eleven times

Clockwise from top left:

The leading soprano Agnes Nicholls made seven appearances between 1902 and 1907. She also sang in the first performance of Wagner's Ring in English. She was married to the composer and conductor Hamilton Harty

The tenor Lloyd Chandos, (sixty-six appearances, 1895–1908), sang everything from Wagner to 'The Death of Nelson'

Gervase Elwes (twenty-seven appearances, 1903–20), was a noted English concert tenor, a famous Gerontius, and the first interpreter of Vaughan Williams's On Wenlock Edge

The Irish bass-baritone Harry Plunket Greene was a leading interpreter of the German Lied and English song (many of Stanford's were written for him). He sang the Songs of the Fleet in October 1914

The American Wagnerian soprano Susan Strong, who made three appearances in 1907-8. She settled in London, and after her retirement from the stage opened a laundry in Baker Street where her customers knew her as Brünnhilde. She sang Senta's Ballad from The Flying Dutchman at the Proms

wife Olga, whom he married in 1898, and was several years in advance of the craze for all things Russian that followed the appearance of the Dyagilev ballet.

Over the following decade, some of the composers introduced at the Proms included Bax, Havergal Brian, Frank Bridge, Busoni, Debussy, Delius, Fauré, Mahler, Musorgsky, Rakhmaninov, Ravel, Reger, Sibelius, Ethel Smyth, Josef Suk and Ralph Vaughan Williams.

Henry Wood was always keen on giving opportunities to young performers, and spent an enormous amount of time auditioning. Many of the names to be found in his early programmes have faded into oblivion, but there are some startling surprises as well: the nine Prom performances given in 1901 by the seventeen-year-old Wilhelm Backhaus, for example. In 1908 Myra Hess, aged eighteen, played Liszt's E flat Piano Concerto – the first of her ninety-two appearances at the Proms. Her cousin Irene Scharrer appeared regularly for forty years after her Prom debut in 1905 at the age of eighteen. Of the 105 soloists engaged for the 1914 season, a sensation was caused by the eleven-year-old Solomon, who was also to have a Prom career of forty years.

Queen's Hall, 1907

23

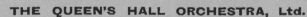

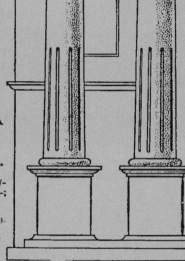

Sir Arthur Sullivan c1895. In 1901, the year following his death, a memorial Prom was devoted to a programme of his serious and popular works

'RAISING THE STANDARD...'

Wood was a man of broad musical tastes and sympathies, and a great deal of his success was due to his understanding of the tastes and sympathies of his audiences. If anything went wrong he wanted to know why. As late as the mid-1930s, having conducted Elgar's *Falstaff* in front of a disappointingly cool audience, he then spent the interval among the Promenaders anxiously trying to find out why this masterpiece had not been more of an attraction.

Neither a bohemian on the one hand, nor a frequenter of aristocratic salons on the other, he remained all his life a solid middle-class Londoner, but without any trace of insularity. Although devoted to good music of all styles and nations, his promotion of British composers and performers helped to overcome a deep prejudice of the period. The patriotism of the Edwardian era did not necessarily extend to musical matters. What we now call the English Musical Renaissance was in full swing, but the majority of music-lovers were still convinced that real musicians had to be foreign, and preferably German.

Wood's energy and dedication were phenomenal. He personally rehearsed and conducted everything, except when he invited composers to conduct their own music, or on the rare occasions when he allowed a guest conductor to appear. (It should be remembered that the Proms occupied only two months of the year, and that Henry Wood was no less busy for the remaining ten.)

The conditions under which the early Proms were prepared sound horrifying by modern standards. There were only three rehearsals a week, each lasting three hours, to cover six concerts. The orchestral players were at first paid forty-five shillings (£2.25) for each week's rehearsals and concerts, although Wood soon managed to increase their fees.

It might be thought that under such conditions the standard of playing could never rise to great heights, but that was apparently not the case at all. A performance in September 1898 of Tchaikovsky's Fifth Symphony elicited this letter from Sir Arthur Sullivan:

Dear Mr. Wood,
 I have a fairly long experience of orchestral playing and orchestral

Below: The pianist Solomon broadcasting for the BBC in 1950. As a child prodigy, Solomon first played at the Proms in 1914, returning on seventy-three occasions over the next forty-one years

Wood as seen by Vanity Fair *in 1907*

Friday's sacred to Beethoven. You must please attend, I beg, on
Twenty-ninth September, when that master-pianist Petri (Egon)
Plays the fourth P.F. Concerto; you should also not be slow in
Hearing Lamond, Clifford Curzon, Maurice Cole and Harriet Cohen.
Of the symphonies composed by this undoubtedly great master, all
Are found in the prospectus; don't omit to hear the 'Pastoral'.
And on Friday, 6th October, there's a work you don't hear daily,
Viz., the symphony called 'Choral', with (as soloists) Miss Baillie,
Parry Jones and Harold Williams; and you'll travel far to meet a
More euphonious contralto than Miss Balfour (Marguerita).

from Diogenes's Handy Guide to the Proms (1939 Edition)

London Underground poster advertising
the capital's concert halls, by S. T. C.
Weeks, 1913

FOR MUSIC.

ÆOLIAN HALL -	**Bond Street** or Dover St.	**BECHSTEIN HALL**-Oxford Circus or Bond Street
ALBERT HALL -	**S. Kensington.**	**STEINWAY HALL** - Marble Arch or Bond Street
QUEEN'S HALL -	**Oxford Circus.**	

Everybody has his own particular
recollections of the Queen's Hall
Proms., but certain memories will be
common to all. These will certainly
include Sir Henry's carnation; his
invariable glance to left and right
before the first upward movement of
the stick; his momentary disappear-
ance from the platform, to reappear
dragging with him at arm's length a
lady vocalist – the effect being so
suggestive of two vessels attached by
a hawser that some wit called it 'The Queen's Haul'; the fountain in the Promenade; people faint-
ing on a sultry evening (less often after the new air-conditioning plant was installed in 1937)
and being quietly looked after by the St John Ambulance men; the imperturbable accompanist,
organist and player of the celesta, Frederick B. Kiddle; the old gentleman who used to play the
cymbals and who could be seen getting ready for a mighty clash, afterwards relaxing with quiet
satisfaction at a vital task successfully accomplished [...]

Robert Elkin, Queen's Hall 1893–1941 [1944]

Lionel Tertis in 1934. Though the celebrated viola player turned down the 1929 premiere of Walton's Concerto, he played it two years later in one of his eight solo appearances at the Proms

conducting, and I say quite sincerely that I have never heard a finer performance in England than that of the Tchaikovsky Symphony under your direction last Wednesday.

It was a perfect delight to listen to such accent, phrasing, delicacy and force, and I congratulate both the gifted conductor, and the splendid orchestra. And what a lovely work it is! I could see that you and the band, too, revelled in bringing out its beauties.

Wood was unfailingly considerate towards the ill-paid and over-worked orchestral musicians, but a serious crisis came in 1904 when he determined to put an end once and for all to the deputy system – the practice by which orchestral players could send substitutes to rehearsals, appearing in person only for the concert. Around fifty members of the Queen's Hall Orchestra refused to accept the new conditions and went on to form the nucleus of the London Symphony Orchestra. The leader of Wood's viola section, Lionel Tertis, took this opportunity to leave the orchestra and develop his distinguished solo career, which included several Proms appearances until 1947, often playing works written especially for him, such as Walton's Viola Concerto and Vaughan Williams's *Flos campi*.

If many problems could be dealt with by energy and determination, others could be cured only by money. After the turn of the century, the financial problems became increasingly acute. Robert Newman had been extending his activities to the unpredictable world of the theatre, and had soon found himself seriously in debt, unable any longer to support the orchestra. He remained only as manager of the hall. A syndicate was formed under the direction of the German-born banker Sir Edgar Speyer, an enlightened patron of the arts and friend of Elgar. The lease of the hall was taken over by the music publishers Chappell and Co. The style of the Proms, however, remained largely unchanged. Wood's services to music were recognised with a knighthood in 1911. Although he now became 'Sir Henry' to the world in general, to the orchestra he remained 'Timber'.

A 1930s advertisement in Radio Times *by Mabel Lapthorn for Brahms Nights, which were a regular feature at the Proms from the early years*

Brahms Night at the Queen's Hall.

QUEEN'S HALL

Sole Lessees   Messrs. CHAPPELL & Co. Ltd.

THE QUEEN'S HALL ORCHESTRA, Ltd.

Directors:

The Rt. Hon. Sir Edgar Speyer, Bart. (Chairman).
The Earl Howe, G.C.V.O.   The Earl of Londesborough, K.C.V.O.
Sir Henry J. Wood.   John Roskill, Esq., K.C.
H. Egan Hill, Esq.
Secretary   F. Pope.

PROMENADE CONCERTS

20TH SEASON.

AUGUST 15th to OCTOBER 24th, 1914.

Every Evening at 8.   Doors open at 7.30.

MONDAY, AUGUST 31st, 1914, at 8.

Miss VIOLET OPPENSHAW.

Mr. ROBERT RADFORD.

THE QUEEN'S HALL ORCHESTRA.

Principal Violin   -   -   Mr. ARTHUR CATTERALL.
Organist & Accompanist   Mr. FREDK. B. KIDDLE.
Conductor   -   Sir HENRY J. WOOD.

Promenade, 1/-; Balcony, 2/-; Grand Circle (numbered and reserved), 3/- & 5/-. SEASON TICKETS (Transferable), available till October 23rd—Promenade, 21/-; Balcony, 63/-; Grand Circle, 4½ and 5 Guineas.
Smoking Permitted (except in the portion of Grand Circle reserved for non-smokers).
THE QUEEN'S HALL ORCHESTRA, Ltd., 320 Regent Street, W.

Telephone—551 Paddington.   ROBERT NEWMAN, Manager.
Telegram: "Accompany, Wesdo, London"

THE FIRST WORLD WAR

The twentieth season coincided with the outbreak of World War I. There were doubts whether the Proms could continue at all in wartime conditions, but Robert Newman would have none of them: 'Why not? The war can't last three months and the public will need its music and, incidentally, our orchestra its salaries'. The War lasted considerably more than three months, but the Proms went on regardless, even if there had to be some changes of emphasis.

Almost overnight, all things German became anathema. Wood and Newman together tactfully countered the anti-Hun fury which threatened so much of their repertory, wisely insisting that 'The greatest examples of Music and Art are world possessions and unassailable even by the prejudices and passions of the hour'. As George Bernard Shaw acidly commented, 'In London last August the usual series of nightly cheap orchestral concerts called Promenade Concerts announced patriotically that no German music would be performed. Everybody applauded the announcement. But nobody went to the concerts. Within a week a programme full of Beethoven, Wagner and Strauss was announced. Everybody was shocked; and everybody went to the concert. It was a complete and decisive German victory, with nobody killed'.

There was one notable casualty, however: Sir Edgar Speyer, disgracefully, was hounded out of the country early in 1915 and Chappell's took over the running of the orchestra as well as the lease of the hall. In accordance with the spirit of the times, the flags of the allied nations hung in the auditorium, and their national anthems were

BBC

George Bernard Shaw, music critic turned playwright, maintained a keen interest in activities at the Queen's Hall

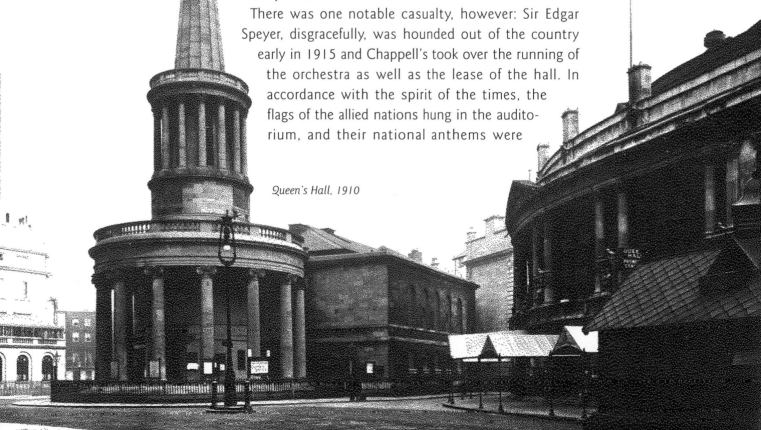

Queen's Hall, 1910

QUEEN'S HALL ORCHESTRA, LTD.

Directors:

THE RT. HON. SIR EDGAR SPEYER, BART., *Chairman.*

THE EARL HOWE, G.C.V.O.   THE EARL OF LONDESBOROUGH, K.C.V.O.

SIR HENRY J. WOOD.   JOHN ROSKILL, ESQ., K.C.

H. EGAN HILL, ESQ.

Secretary • • • F. POPE.

TELEGRAMS: "ACCOMPANY WESDO, LONDON."
TELEPHONE: 551 PADDINGTON.

Manager:
ROBERT NEWMAN.

Offices:

320 Regent Street, W.

The Directors of the Queen's Hall Orchestra think that some explanation of the change of programme on Monday evening, August 17th, is due to their Subscribers and to all who have so loyally supported the Promenade Concerts in the past. The substitution of a mixed programme in place of a wholly Wagnerian one was not dictated by any narrow-minded intolerant policy, but was the result of outside pressure brought to bear upon them at the eleventh hour by the Lessees of the Queen's Hall.

With regard to the future, the Directors hope—with the broad-minded co-operation of their audience—to carry through as nearly as possible the original scheme of the Concerts as set forth in their Prospectus.

They take this opportunity of emphatically contradicting the statements that German music will be boycotted during the present season. The greatest examples of Music and Art are world possessions and unassailable even by the prejudices and passions of the hour.

For the Directors of the Queen's Hall Orchestra,

ROBERT NEWMAN,
Manager.

Nowadays we regard Béla Bartók as one of the leading forces in the development of modern music, but his works were unknown in England until 1914. On September 1 we played his suite for orchestra for the first time. This very original Hungarian composer's idiom was somewhat strange and brought forth a protest from one or two members of the orchestra who objected to 'playing such stuff' during the war – the only time, as far as I can remember, I ever received a complaint of the kind. I recall with amusement that A. E. Brain – brother of Aubrey Brain, our present leader of the horns – stood up and 'went for' me.

'Surely you can find better novelties than this kind of stuff?' he said indignantly. I saw there was a call for a little tact.

'You must remember', I said, 'that I must interpret all schools of music – much that I do not really care for – but I never want my feelings to reflect upon my orchestra. You never know, but I am of opinion this man will take a prominent position one day. It may take him years to establish it, but his originality and idiom mark his music as the type of novelty our public ought to hear.' This calmed Brain and, moreover, I have had the satisfaction of seeing my prediction fulfilled.

Henry J. Wood, My Life of Music *(1938)*

An announcement by Robert Newman inserted into the programme for 21 August 1914. The following Monday saw a return to the usual Wagner Night

Robert Radford at the Handel Festival in 1906. A popular oratorio singer as well as a member of the Beecham Opera Company and later the British National Opera Company, the English bass sang on fifty occasions at the Proms between 1902 and 1927. During the First World War he contributed patriotic items such as 'There's Only One England' and 'Old England's a Lion'

played before every concert in 1914 and 1915 ('untold boredom', remarked Wood, who had to prepare the orchestrations).

The German classics were safe, but when it came to 'novelties', the composers were all from the Allied countries – principally Britain, France, Italy and Russia. New music by 'enemy aliens' had to wait until 1919. One notable Saturday evening Prom in 1915, a mixed Scandinavian and French programme, was conducted by Mr Thomas Beecham – his first Prom appearance, and also his last until 1954. Sadly, there was little love lost between the two great English conductors of their day. Both eventually wrote autobiographies in which the other is not even mentioned. There is a legendary report of a conversation between the two, in which Beecham marvelled at Wood's energy. 'I just don't know how you do it – it would kill me.' 'Yes', replied Wood.

The wartime conditions did have two very positive side-effects: the lack of foreign soloists brought into relief the great amount of native musical talent, while the ravages of conscription on the orchestra led to an increasing number of women players being engaged. Apart from the harp, traditionally a ladies' instrument, orchestras had until then been heavily male preserves, although as early as 1913 Wood had been encouraging what Ethel Smyth referred to as 'mixed bathing in the sea of music'.

> *To-morrow we have the Second Symphony of Beethoven, which I have been reading about in the book you lent me. The thing to look out for is evidently a bit near the end. 'Earth is forgotten and we are in Heaven,' the book says: so I shall expect something with a plus handicap there. [...] Topping concert. I spotted the bit near the end all right [...] – simply ripping. The second movement was also top-hole (i.e. the one after the first pause – there is an introduction before the first movement, but it goes straight on): it begins, dum, dum, dum, dum, quite quiet: then dum dumti-dumti-dumti, getting a bit of a move on; then dum-diddle-iddle-um-tum-tum; dum-diddle-iddle-um-tum-tum; dum-diddle-iddle-um-tum-tum; dum-diddle-iddle-umti-dumti-dumti-dum.*
>
> 'J. R. Harrison',
> *from* The Promenade Ticket: a lay record of concert-going (1914) *by A. H. Sidgwick*

Harpists of the BBC Symphony Orchestra: Jeanne Chevreau (left) and Sidonie Goossens

On Saturday, you take what comes
And trust to luck to find some plums;
A little bit of everything,
Where roundabout makes up for swing.
(Handel, Tchaikovsky, Stanford, Gounod,
Sibelius, Schubert, Saint-Saëns – you know.)
Now, reader, if you've paid good heed
I've told you everything you need.
You know now what you'll have to face
Next time you go to Langham Place.

'Diogenes the Younger',
Guide to the 'Proms', Musical Opinion (1929)

Below: Wood in action. A montage
of drawings of the conductor made
in 1938 by Enoch Fairhurst

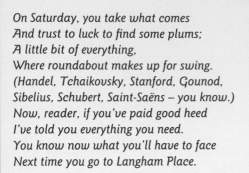

THE
PROMENADE CONCERTS
BY UNDERGROUND
TO OXFORD CIRCUS

London Underground poster by Fred Taylor (1920) advertising the Proms

King George V and Queen Mary (in balcony, top left)
visit the Proms in 1924

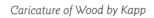

Caricature of Wood by Kapp

BETWEEN THE WARS: ENTER THE BBC

Photographs and newsreels of the postwar years evoke Flappers and Bright Young Things, cocktails, jazz and cloche hats. They also show mutilated ex-soldiers selling matches in the street, mass unemployment and the General Strike. What did Sir Henry Wood have in common with such a world? Not very much. Wood was oblivious to almost everything outside the world of music. In brief periods of relaxation, he painted. There is no record of him ever having read a newspaper.

Whatever upheavals were going on in the land fit for heroes, the demand for music was unchanged, and the Queen's Hall (now re-decorated in a rather shocking bluish-green) was always full for the summer Promenade Concerts. Wood continued to ensure an enterprising mixture of the familiar and the new. The 1920 season, for example, contained eighteen novelties, of which eight were first performances. Among the artists appearing for the first time were the pianist Harriet Cohen (playing Bax's Symphonic Variations) and the violinist Jelly d'Arányi (playing the Beethoven concerto). Both were to appear regularly in the following years, as would the sisters May and Beatrice Harrison. In 1922 Wood introduced some music by Monteverdi, practically unknown in those days, and in 1923 the twenty-two novelties included the first British performance of Saint-Saëns's *Carnival of the Animals*. This season marked the first Prom appearances of the singers Isobel Baillie and Astra Desmond.

Unfortunately, financial problems were again becoming pressing. The Proms were running at a loss, and a further blow came with the death of Robert Newman in 1926. Rising costs affected all aspects of concert-giving, and in the following year Chappell's announced that they were no longer in a position to support the Proms.

Wood issued a statement to the press, thanking Chappell's for what they had achieved, and the large financial sacrifices they had made. By now, however, the Proms had become a national institution (they had been graced by a royal visit in 1924). With over thirty years of tradition behind him Wood could state with some confidence, 'It would be a disgrace to this country if the

Wood the amateur painter

Ida Haendel in 1938, the year after her Prom debut. The great Polish-born violinist has remained a popular soloist at the Proms over more than fifty seasons

It is good to be back at the Promenades again – to see the same old notice asking us to refrain from STRIKING MATCHES (this is all that is visible), the same old fountain in the middle, which will be removed when London fills up towards the time of the Pastoral Symphony, and the same old band of enthusiasts having the first hole punched in their season tickets. The young man with the wild hair and the large score under his arm is here again, and the swan-necked Adonis with his three dowdy adorers, and the hard-favoured solitary in a bowler hat who never moves a muscle and never misses a concert. I cannot find the ecstatic couple who clutch each other at the entrance of their favourite themes, but no doubt they are at the seaside, and will return before long.

'Nigel F. Clarke',
from The Promenade Ticket:
a lay record of concert-going (1914) by
A. H. Sidgwick

Wood in rehearsal at Queen's Hall on 1 October 1938

ROYAL ALBERT HALL

JUBILEE

"PROMS"

SEASON

Poster advertising the Jubilee season of the Proms in 1944

Wood conducts the BBC Symphony Orchestra at the Proms in August 1933. More than sixty years later, the orchestra continues to provide the backbone of the season

Percy Pitt (1869–1932). A wide-ranging musician, he had worked as Wood's pianist and organist at the Queen's Hall before becoming a conductor himself. Later, as the BBC's first Director of Music, he was able to provide the necessary financial support to ensure the Proms' future

'Promenades' were to go. But we have done so much that I am sure that we are going to do a great deal more. The education that has been given to the public is going to tell, and the help given by broadcasting and by very fine gramophone records is, I am sure, going to bear very great fruit in the future'.

As Newman had wished, shortly before his death, the answer was indeed to be found in the new medium of broadcasting. In 1927 the British Broadcasting Company, under its Director John Reith, had become a Corporation with the mandate 'to inform, educate and entertain'. After intricate negotiations, the BBC agreed to take over the Proms. Wood was left in sole charge of programmes – essentially, the best of the classic orchestral repertory, with a mixture of lighter items and carefully chosen 'novelties'. The BBC, mindful of box-office receipts, was more cautious about allowing new music than Wood, left entirely to himself, would have wished, but he seems to have had his own way most of the time. The more trivial items to be found in earlier programmes – the ballads and Grand Fantasias – had by now disappeared altogether, the orchestral players were better paid, and more generous rehearsal time (daily, rather than only three rehearsals a week) allowed much more detailed preparation of the music. Wood could also obtain extra players if they were needed for larger works. He could rely on at least one firm ally in the BBC – Percy Pitt, the Director of Music, had been engaged as pianist and organist for the Proms in 1896, and for many years had accompanied the solo songs as well as taking the celesta part in the innumerable performances of the *Nutcracker* Suite.

The name of the orchestra had to change. The original 'Queen's Hall Orchestra' of 1895 had become 'The New Queen's Hall Orchestra' when managed by Chappell's, and they would not allow the BBC to continue using this name. For three seasons the Proms were therefore performed by 'Sir Henry Wood and his Symphony Orchestra'. This situation lasted until 1930, when the orchestra merged with the London Wireless Orchestra to form the ninety-strong BBC Symphony Orchestra, whose first Principal Conductor was Adrian Boult.

From 1927, broadcasting opened the Proms to a far wider audience. Some people at the time, particularly William Boosey, Managing Director of

The Opening Night of the 1936 season is under way. Soloist Arthur Fear is singing (in English) 'The term is past' ('Die Frist ist um') from The Flying Dutchman

Wood's scores and parts arrive at the Queen's Hall in time for the 1935 Prom season. The secret of Wood's ability to rehearse so much material quickly lay in the meticulously prepared marked-up parts he gave to his players.

On the far left is Bill Edwards (1913–95) who retired as Orchestral Supervisor of the BBC SO in 1978. For forty-six of his fifty years at the BBC he worked for the orchestra

Making music at home: Wood and his daughters Tania (cello) and Avril (piano)

A preoccupied cellist passes Queen's Hall in a 1930 London Underground advertisement by Charles Pears

The Musician travels UNDERGROUND

The hall (with fountain in the Arena) awaits the Promenaders: August 1928

BBC

Dame Ethyl Smyth broadcasting in June 1928. Wood supported Smyth's music loyally over the years, giving several first concert performances of excerpts from her operas at the Proms. He would have been pleased to know of the revival of her masterpiece The Wreckers in the 1994 season

BBC

Dame Ethel is a law unto herself and given, like many composers, to making last-minute suggestions. Sometimes Dame Ethel goes further than last-minute suggestions: she makes last-minute alterations. I remember going with Lady Speyer and Lady Maud Warrender to hear The Wreckers at His Majesty's. We arrived at 2.15 for the 2.30 matinée. I said: 'Where's Ethel Smyth? I don't see her anywhere. It's a wonder she hasn't been down into the orchestral pit by now to make a few alterations in the band parts.'

She would never do that as late as this,' said Lady Speyer. 'It is nearly twenty-past two.' 'I don't care,' I said. 'She will be there with her little slips to pin on.' 'I don't believe it.' 'All right. I'll bet you a pound she does.' 'Done!' We waited.

Sure enough, at 2.25 the composer appeared, stealing in through the iron door, and proceeded to affix alterations over certain brass parts. I was jubilant. 'I don't suppose she has told the conductor, either,' I said. 'He will wonder what on earth is happening when he comes to the passage. Now what about that pound you owe me?' Lady Speyer paid up.

Henry J. Wood, My Life of Music (1938)

(incl   E (reserved) 5/- 6/- 7/6
SEASON TICKETS (Promenade—a limited number) :   Whole Series 37/6
(including Tax)   First or last four weeks 21/-

THE ILLUSTRATED LONDON NEWS PICTURE LIBRARY

Moura Lympany, who first played in 1938, returned most recently in the 1994 season with her fourth Prom performance of the Second Concerto of Rakhmaninov, a composer who is one of her specialities. In all she has made sixty appearances

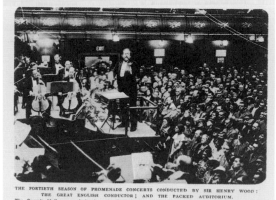

THE FORTIETH SEASON OF PROMENADE CONCERTS CONDUCTED BY SIR HENRY WOOD; THE GREAT ENGLISH CONDUCTOR; AND THE PACKED AUDITORIUM.

The Queen's Hall was packed when the Fortieth Season of Promenade Concerts conducted by Sir Henry Wood opened there on August 11. Sir Henry himself received a tremendous ovation. Both Elgar and Holst were represented in the programme, the former by the Prelude to "The Kingdom," the latter by three of "The Planets," Strauss's "Till Eulenspiegel" and Rimsky-Korsakov's "Capriccio Espagnol" were also given; and Miss Maggie Teyte sang Mimi's air from "La Bohème."

The fortieth season opened on 18 August 1934. The evening's soloists were Maggie Teyte, baritone Dennis Noble and pianist Irene Kohler

Chappell's, feared that radio listening might kill off live concert-going, but Henry Wood (now with a microphone suspended above his head as he conducted) did not agree. 'With the wholehearted support of the wonderful medium of broadcasting, I feel that I am at last on the threshold of realising my life-long ambition of truly democratising the message of music, and making its beneficent effect universal … I am quite convinced that not only in music, but generally, the medium of broadcasting, as utilised and developed in this country, is one of the few elements ordinarily associated with the progress of civilisation which I can heartily endorse.'

STUART-LIFF COLLECTION

The popular Australian bass-baritone Peter Dawson, who probably made more recordings than any other artist, sang popular ballads and operatic solos at the Proms between 1904 and 1935. He introduced the famous ballad Boots, written by him under the pseudonym J. P. McCall, at the Proms. Wood thought it 'common'

Below: *Maggie Teyte, much admired as Mélisande (by Debussy amongst others), and in French song as well as musical comedy, sang at the Proms between 1922 and 1935, including works by Debussy, Ravel, and regularly the Letter Scene from* Eugene Onegin

The 1927 season of six weeks observed the following scheme, which was to remain in its essentials the pattern for many years: Monday meant Wagner and Friday meant Beethoven; Tuesday featured Haydn and Mozart, Wednesday Brahms or Bach (Myra Hess's performances of the keyboard concertos were always great attractions); Thursday would feature a mixture of composers, and the most unusual items of a week's programming would appear here. Saturday nights (always sold out) would be devoted to lighter, popular programmes.

The roster of artists, both British and foreign, continued to be impressive. In 1928, Zoltán Kodály came to conduct his *Háry János Suite*; the following year Paul Hindemith introduced Walton's Viola Concerto; in 1931 Francis Poulenc played his *Aubade*; in 1933 Joseph Szigeti played the violin concertos of Brahms and Beethoven, and Samuel Dushkin performed the Violin Concerto Stravinsky had recently written for him. Eva Turner made her Prom debut in 1934, and in 1936 there were two appearances by Artur Rubinstein.

As always, Wood remained on the lookout for good new music from abroad; but perhaps the greatest achievements of the Proms in the late 1920s and 1930s were in British music. There was hardly any British composer of significance who failed to have a piece introduced at the Proms during this period, and many were invited to conduct or play their own music: among them were Vaughan Williams, Holst, Bridge, Bliss, Walton, Warlock, Berkeley and Lambert. One of Elgar's last compositions, his *Nursery Suite*, was premiered at the Proms in 1931, and in 1933, just six months before his death, he made his final appearance conducting his Second Symphony. In 1938 the young Benjamin Britten made his Prom debut playing the solo part of his new Piano Concerto.

STUART-LIFF COLLECTION

Joseph Hislop was Britain's leading international tenor during the 1920s and 1930s. He appeared on thirteen occasions at the Proms, with Puccini and Eric Coates figuring frequently in his selections

STUART-LIFF COLLECTION

Eva Turner, a dramatic soprano and a famous Turandot, used to complain to Wood that the Wagner extracts she sang at the Proms gave little idea of the scope of her repertoire. 'No-one sings them like you', Wood disarmingly replied. Later, as Dame Eva Turner, the former opera star was a keen attender at the Proms up to the end of her long life

Below: *Wood surveys the ruins of the Queen's Hall after it had been destroyed by enemy bombing. To make the shot seem more 'heroic', two members of the BBC staff accompanying Wood were removed from the photo (see opposite page)*

AN AIR-RAID WARNING HAS BEEN RECEIVED THE CONCERT WILL CONTINUE BUT THOSE WISHING TO LEAVE MAY DO SO

SIR HENRY WOOD vs. THE LUFTWAFFE

Friday 1 September 1939 was Beethoven Night at the Proms. It was also the date of Hitler's invasion of Poland. The BBC had the unenviable task of explaining certain national priorities to Wood. At the end of the 'Pastoral' Symphony, he reluctantly addressed the audience: 'Owing to the special arrangements for broadcasting which are now in force, the BBC very much regrets that the Symphony Orchestra will no longer be available for these concerts in London. I am therefore very sorry to say that from tonight the Promenade Concerts will close down until further notice'. The BBC's evacuation plans went into immediate effect: the Music Department, including the Symphony Orchestra, was moved first to Bristol, and then to Bedford.

With Wood are Hubert Clifford (left, BBC Empire Music Director) and John Gough (right, BBC Pacific Programmes Organiser)

The Queen's Hall was right next-door to Broadcasting House, a prime target for air-raids; but the Proms had survived one war, and Wood was determined that nothing should prevent them continuing through another. With single-minded persistence he sought ways of preserving the Proms in one form or another. If the BBC was unable to support them, other ways would have to be found. After long negotiations, Wood eventually entered into a partnership with a private sponsor, Keith Douglas, and arranged an eight-week season for the summer of 1940. The London Symphony Orchestra would replace the BBC Symphony Orchestra. In the event, only four weeks of this season could be given: the Blitz proved too much even for the Proms.

The last Queen's Hall Prom was given on Saturday 7 September 1940. This concert seems typical of what Henry Wood might consider

[Malcolm Sargent became a regular conductor at the Proms in 1947, and was Chief Conductor from 1950 until his death in 1967. He had first appeared in 1921, conducting his own work An Impression on a Windy Day. It was on 10 May 1941 that he conducted Elgar's The Dream of Gerontius, the last performance to take place at Queen's Hall, before its destruction by an incendiary bomb a few hours later.]

On the morning of Monday, May 12, 1941, I was taken round the charred remains of my beloved concert hall by Mr Taylor, the manager. It was a sad but strangely macabre sight. Nothing was left within the walls of the auditorium but rusty metal. It might have been the remains of an iron foundry or the site of an old refuse heap. Two great tanks from the roof had crashed into the arena, the organ pipes had melted, the floor of the circle was strewn with thousands of springs from the seats of the chairs. I was much moved, and found that I had instinctively taken off my hat.

We talked of many concerts, of great music and musicians, of unforgettable happinesses within its walls. I tried to visualise the many occasions on which I had conducted there in the twenty years between 1921 and 1941, but chiefly I remembered my happiest moments in the empty hall. After a morning rehearsal I loved best to return in the afternoon to the dimly lit building and, sitting at the back of the circle, or pacing up and down the centre gangway, meditate upon my evening's music. One felt the spirit of the building breathing echoes of past beauty as an empty cathedral whispers sanctity.

Malcolm Sargent, Foreword to Robert Elkin, Queen's Hall 1893–1941 [1944]

Above: Wood conducting the London Symphony Orchestra
at the Proms in 1941

BBC

The date is 24 July 1943.
Wood conducted his famous
arrangement (by 'Paul Klenovsky')
of Bach's Toccata and Fugue in
D minor for the last time in
this Prom

Wood with associate conductors Adrian Boult (left) and Basil Cameron (right) on 1 August 1942

Wood's score of Beethoven's Seventh Symphony, the last work he conducted. Boult said of this final performance, 'It swept us along with all the torrential energy of that immortal work'

a good mixed programme: among the nine items of nineteenth- and twentieth-century music there were arias by Delibes and Puccini, music by Holbrooke and Bax, Rakhmaninov's Second Piano Concerto played by Moiseiwitsch, and – a tough novelty – the first performance of Elisabeth Lutyens's Three Pieces for Orchestra.

The Queen's Hall survived for a further eight months until 10 May 1941. On that night London suffered one of the worst bombardments of the War. There were direct hits on Westminster Abbey, the British Museum, the Law Courts, the Tower and the War Office. The House of Commons Chamber was destroyed, and the Queen's Hall was totally gutted by fire. The curious may still inspect a tiny piece of wall in an alley off Great Portland Street – all that remains standing today of this wonderful building. Photographed amidst the debris, Wood strikes a 'bloody but unbowed' attitude.

The only building in London which could still be used for orchestral concerts was the Royal Albert Hall in South Kensington. Opened in 1871, it was originally going to be called simply 'Hall of Arts and Sciences', but Queen Victoria had unexpectedly (if predictably) added the prefix 'Royal Albert' when laying the foundation stone. After seventy years, its original grandeur was somewhat decayed, and it certainly lacked the intimacy of Queen's Hall; but it was available, and it was large – with a capacity of 6,500 it was well over twice the size of the Queen's Hall. It has proved a worthy enough setting for the Proms' second half-century – indeed, for many people, 'Proms' and 'Albert Hall' are virtually synonymous. For a long time it suffered from the drawback of poor acoustics, sluggish and with an echo so prolonged that it was said to be the only place in London where a British composer was likely to hear his work performed twice. Screens were at first erected to improve the acoustics, although the worst of the problems were only solved in 1968 with the suspension of the 'flying saucer' acoustic dishes from the roof.

The Royal Albert Hall began its Prom career with a season of six weeks in the summer of 1941. For the first time, the

From the 1942 season

1942

Poster for the fiftieth season of Promenade Concerts in 1944

The brilliant composer, conductor and writer Constant Lambert (1905–51), who first conducted at the Proms in 1929, appearing regularly in the last years of his life

There is a masculine strength [...] about Constant Lambert, that is one of the first impressions he makes on you; broad shoulders and a fine torso, a large head and an expansive forehead, an alert face on which humour plays a number of good tunes, but on which, now and then, there settles a kind of stern gloom, not to be dispersed by any insensitive back-slapping. He is a too familiar figure in our musical life to need any 'biography' in these pages. You see him conducting ballet at Covent Garden, a studio concert at the People's Palace, Sibelius at the Proms, recording at Maida Vale, reciting the Sitwell poems in Façade at the Lyric, Hammersmith, playing billiards with a friend, lunching at Pagani's, discussing railways and railway engines in the 'local', laughing in the street over the latest quips in 'Beachcomber', arguing about pictures with Michael Ayrton, discussing the atom bomb with a couple of journalists, chewing the cud of a new score with Alan Rawsthorne, exchanging a funny story with an orchestral player ...

C. B. Rees' 'Personality Corner', in Penguin Music Magazine No. 2, ed. Ralph Hill (1947)

Left: Lennox Berkeley in 1943, when his Symphony No. 1 was premiered at the Proms. He had eight premieres of various kinds between 1929 and 1973

The opening night of the Jubilee season in 1944. The soloist is Parry Jones in the Prize Song from Wagner's The Mastersingers

Ralph Vaughan Williams presents Wood with a volume of tributes from many of the world's leading musicians commemorating his seventy-fifth birthday and the fiftieth Prom season, 3 April 1944

seventy-two-year-old Wood divided the conducting with Basil Cameron: usually Wood conducted the first part of the concerts, Cameron the second. In the following year the BBC was again in control. Concerts were for the first time divided between two orchestras, the BBC Symphony and the London Philharmonic. In addition to Wood and Cameron, several concerts were conducted by Adrian Boult, the regular conductor of the BBC SO.

The volume's dedication to Wood

1944 marked two important anniversaries: the fiftieth year of the Proms, and Henry Wood's seventy-fifth birthday. On 2 March, at the Royal Academy of Music, Wood was presented with an album of 267 pages, each bearing a handwritten tribute from the leading composers, conductors, singers and instrumentalists of the day.

Unfortunately, the menace of flying bombs caused the Proms' Jubilee season to be curtailed after less than three weeks, although further concerts were broadcast from Bedford. By now, however, Wood's phenomenal energies were waning after half-a-century of unremitting overwork. His last concert was on 28 July, when he conducted what was generally considered an outstanding performance of Beethoven's Seventh Symphony. He died three weeks later, on 19 August 1944.

Henry Wood's achievements were well summarised in an obituary by Ernest Newman in *The Sunday Times*:

Stravinsky quotes his Capriccio, *which he played under Wood's baton*

> His great qualities were his thorough mastery of the whole language of music and the whole praxis of conducting, his amazing capacity for work, his conscientiousness, that made him, as a matter of course, do his best for whatever new work fell to him to introduce, and that insatiable interest in the musical activity of all countries, all periods, that for half a century kept his audiences abreast of all that was being done in every country.

Wood conducts Eva Turner in a 1941 Prom

Walton's tribute takes the form of the opening bars of his Viola Concerto, premiered at the Proms in 1929

Bartók quotes his Second Piano Concerto

OYAL ALBERT HALL

Manager: C. S. TAYLOR

THE BBC PRESENTS

58TH SEASON OF

HENRY WOOD

PROMENADE

CONCERTS

I am now at work conducting a fortnight of the famous Henry Wood Promenade Concerts here in London. Every night we have the Albert Hall full – seven thousand people or so, and twelve hundred of them stand for two and a half hours listening to that music after they have stood for perhaps an hour or more outside the building waiting for admission. I love to go to those concerts when I am not conducting, and can watch those young crowds standing on the floor. There is a concentration in the expression of each one of them that shows that they have forgotten whether they are standing or sitting. I took a non-musical friend – a great airman – to a concert last season, and this is what he wrote afterwards: 'I felt much impressed with the Promenade Concert. I had no idea that serious music could call up an atmosphere of such deep fellowship and concentration; a very slight twist would have made it one of devotion'.

Adrian Boult, Talk for the BBC Far East Service (1949), quoted in Boult on Music (1983)

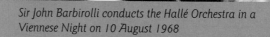

Sir John Barbirolli conducts the Hallé Orchestra in a Viennese Night on 10 August 1968

POSTWAR PROMS IN THE ALBERT HALL

A bronze bust of Sir Henry Wood, rescued from the smouldering ruins of the Queen's Hall, is brought every year from the Royal Academy of Music and placed in front of the organ console in the Albert Hall, where it continues to preside over the Proms. In the absence of the man himself, the character of the Proms was bound to undergo some changes. What is remarkable, though, is how little these changes affected the basic principles Wood had established over half a century. Naturally, the Proms could never again be dominated by a single man, whether administrator or conductor. After 1945, the management, repertory and practical running of the Proms were firmly in the hands of the BBC which, like any large organisation, has always tended to respond to challenges by writing memos and forming committees.

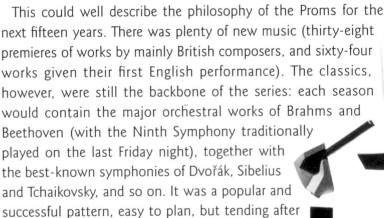

Sir Arthur Bliss, Master of the Queen's Music, draws the ballot for tickets to the First and Last nights of the 1954 season. With him are members of BBC staff and (at the back) C. R. Hopper, Manager of the Royal Albert Hall

The importance of the Proms was never in doubt, but there was much discussion about their exact aims and the nature of the audiences they were directed at – essentially a tug-of-war between those who felt that they should not lose their popular character, vital for attracting new listeners, and those who wished to develop their more substantial 'symphony concert' character. Henry Wood was usually able to strike the correct balance; Victor Hely-Hutchinson, the BBC's Director of Music, showed a certain amount of caution when he concluded after the 1945 season that 'the Promenade audience, though broad-minded and welcoming, is essentially a conservative one, and also that it likes its favourite composers in large doses'.

This could well describe the philosophy of the Proms for the next fifteen years. There was plenty of new music (thirty-eight premieres of works by mainly British composers, and sixty-four works given their first English performance). The classics, however, were still the backbone of the series: each season would contain the major orchestral works of Brahms and Beethoven (with the Ninth Symphony traditionally played on the last Friday night), together with the best-known symphonies of Dvořák, Sibelius and Tchaikovsky, and so on. It was a popular and successful pattern, easy to plan, but tending after

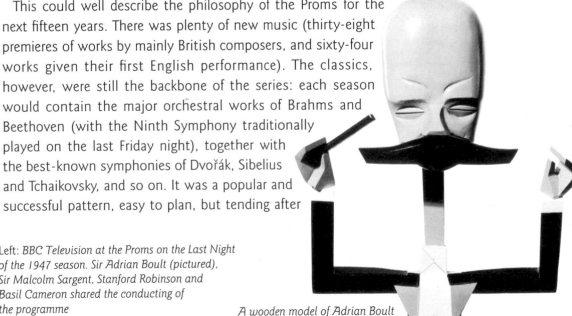

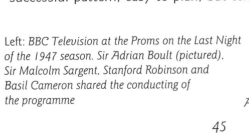

Left: *BBC Television at the Proms on the Last Night of the 1947 season. Sir Adrian Boult (pictured), Sir Malcolm Sargent, Stanford Robinson and Basil Cameron shared the conducting of the programme*

A wooden model of Adrian Boult made in 1934

45

The

Proms

Above: *Michael Tippett (standing) and Adrian Boult. Even under the watchful eye of Boult, the premiere of Tippett's Second Symphony came to grief in February 1958. Happily, the Prom performance that summer was more successful, and the work's appearance in the 1995 season will be its fourth at the Proms*

Right: *Arnold Bax and pianist Harriet Cohen look at the score of Bax's* Concertante for Piano (left hand) and Orchestra, *of which Cohen gave the London premiere at the Proms on 25 July 1950*

THE COMPOSER OF A NEW CONCERTANTE FOR ORCHESTRA AND PIANO (LEFT HAND) AND THE SOLOIST: SIR ARNOLD BAX, MASTER OF THE KING'S MUSICK, AND MISS HARRIET COHEN.

Miss Harriet Cohen was the soloist in Sir Arnold Bax's Concertante for Orchestra and Piano (left hand only), which had its first London performance on July 25 at a Promenade concert. It was written for Miss Cohen, who had a serious accident to her right wrist in 1948.

Far left: *Pianist Mark Hambourg plays Liszt's* Hungarian Fantasy *at the sixtieth-anniversary Prom on 10 August 1954, with Sargent conducting. Hambourg, a pupil of Leschetizky, was born in 1879 and made his Prom debut in 1901. This was his last Prom*

Below left: *Zoltán Kodály rehearsing the BBC Symphony Orchestra in 1946. He conducted his first Prom in 1928, including the UK premiere of his* Háry János Suite, *returning to conduct the same work twenty years later*

Edmund Rubbra rehearsing for the premiere of his Fourth Symphony at the Proms on 14 August 1942

some years to attract criticism for its predictability.

The 1945 season was given by two orchestras, the LSO and BBC SO, and three conductors, Adrian Boult, Basil Cameron and Constant Lambert. All three conductors took part on the Last Night of a season which re-established the Proms on a regular basis after the turmoil of War. Notable events that year were the first British performance of Schoenberg's Piano Concerto and the first Prom appearance of Peter Pears, singing Britten's *Les Illuminations*, conducted by the composer.

After the War the traditional Wagner Nights began to go out of fashion: in 1953, for example, only five concerts featured his music. Various new formats were tried out for the popular Saturday evenings: mixed ballet and opera concerts were introduced in 1950, and Viennese evenings proved highly successful from 1953 onwards. Special occasions and anniversaries were well provided for. 1953 – Coronation year – featured a great deal of British music; in 1957 Kirsten Flagstad emerged from retirement to sing at a concert marking the fiftieth anniversary of Grieg's death. Sibelius's death in that year was marked by performances of all seven of his symphonies during the following season, and Vaughan Williams's death in 1958 was similarly commemorated in 1959 when all nine of his symphonies were played.

The BBC Symphony Orchestra under Malcolm Sargent, its Chief Conductor from 1950, provided the majority of performances; but throughout the 1950s there was a gradual increase in the number of orchestras taking part. The London Symphony Orchestra and the London Philharmonic played regularly. 1953 marked the first visit to the Proms of an orchestra from outside London – the Hallé Orchestra, conducted by Sir John Barbirolli. In the next few years there were performances by the Liverpool Philharmonic and the Bournemouth Symphony Orchestra. 1955 marked the first appearance at the Proms of the National Youth Orchestra. The 1954 Diamond Jubilee season contained two performances by the London Philharmonic conducted by Sir Thomas Beecham, making a return to the Proms after an absence of thirty-nine years.

If any single figure dominated the Proms during this period, it was Sir Malcolm Sargent. His first appearance at a Prom had been as a composer as well as

E. J. Moeran (1894–1950) in 1947. His Serenade for Strings had its premiere at the Proms the following year

Leading light-music composer Eric Coates in 1948. He had played regularly as a violist for Wood, though believed that the conductor disliked his music. Coates nevertheless conducted his own works at the Proms from the 1920s to the 1950s

Below: *Evelyn Rothwell (Lady Barbirolli) with composer Alan Rawsthorne at a rehearsal of his Oboe Concerto, given its first London performance at the Proms in 1947*

The Polish composer Andrzej Panufnik (1914–91) broadcasting an interview on the BBC Polish Service in 1954 with his first wife, Scarlet. He conducted the first concert performance in England of his Sinfonia Rustica *at the Proms the following year*

Right: *1953 Prom poster featuring Sir John Barbirolli*

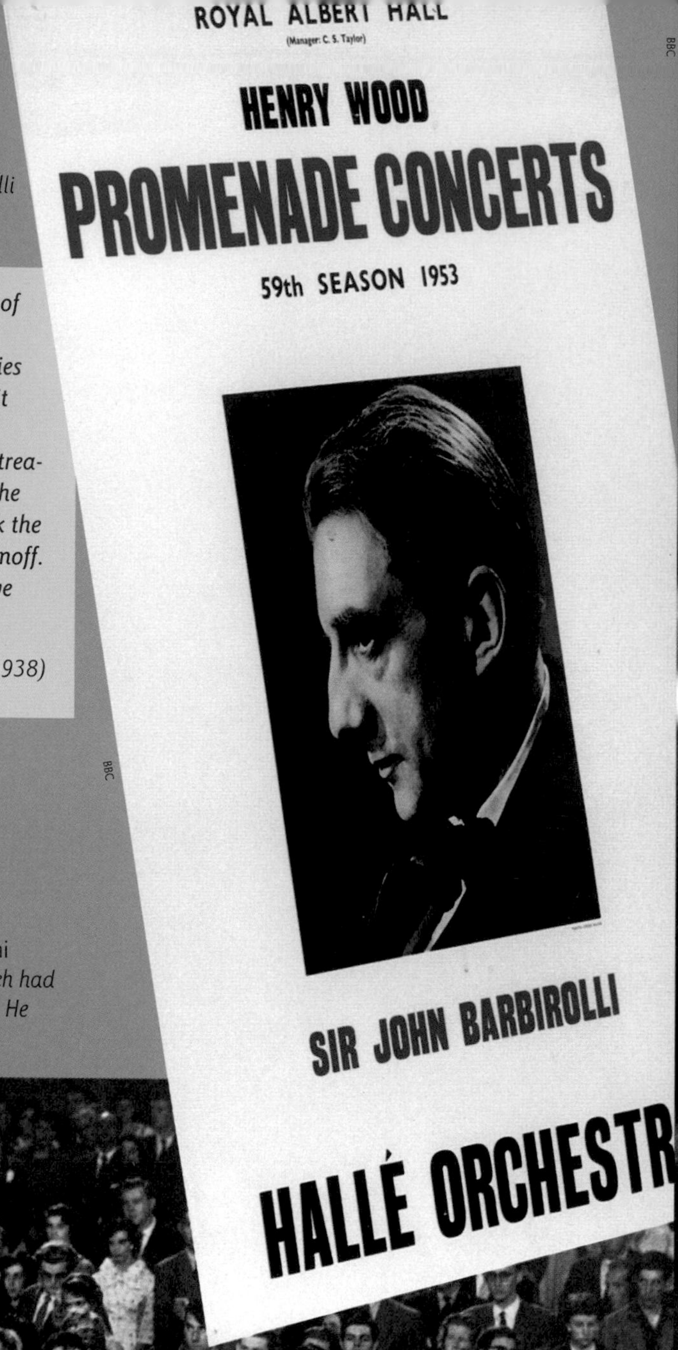

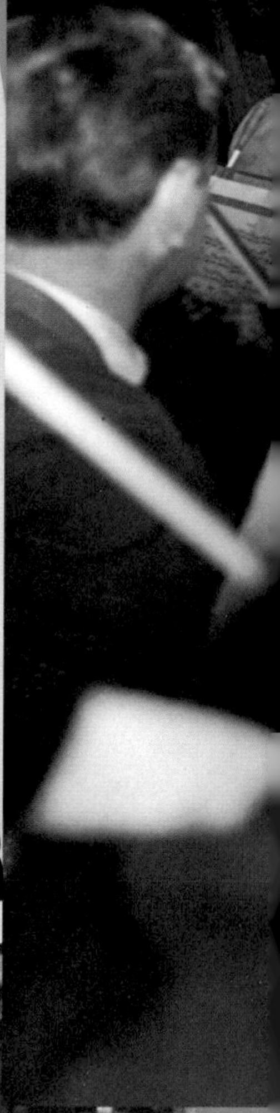

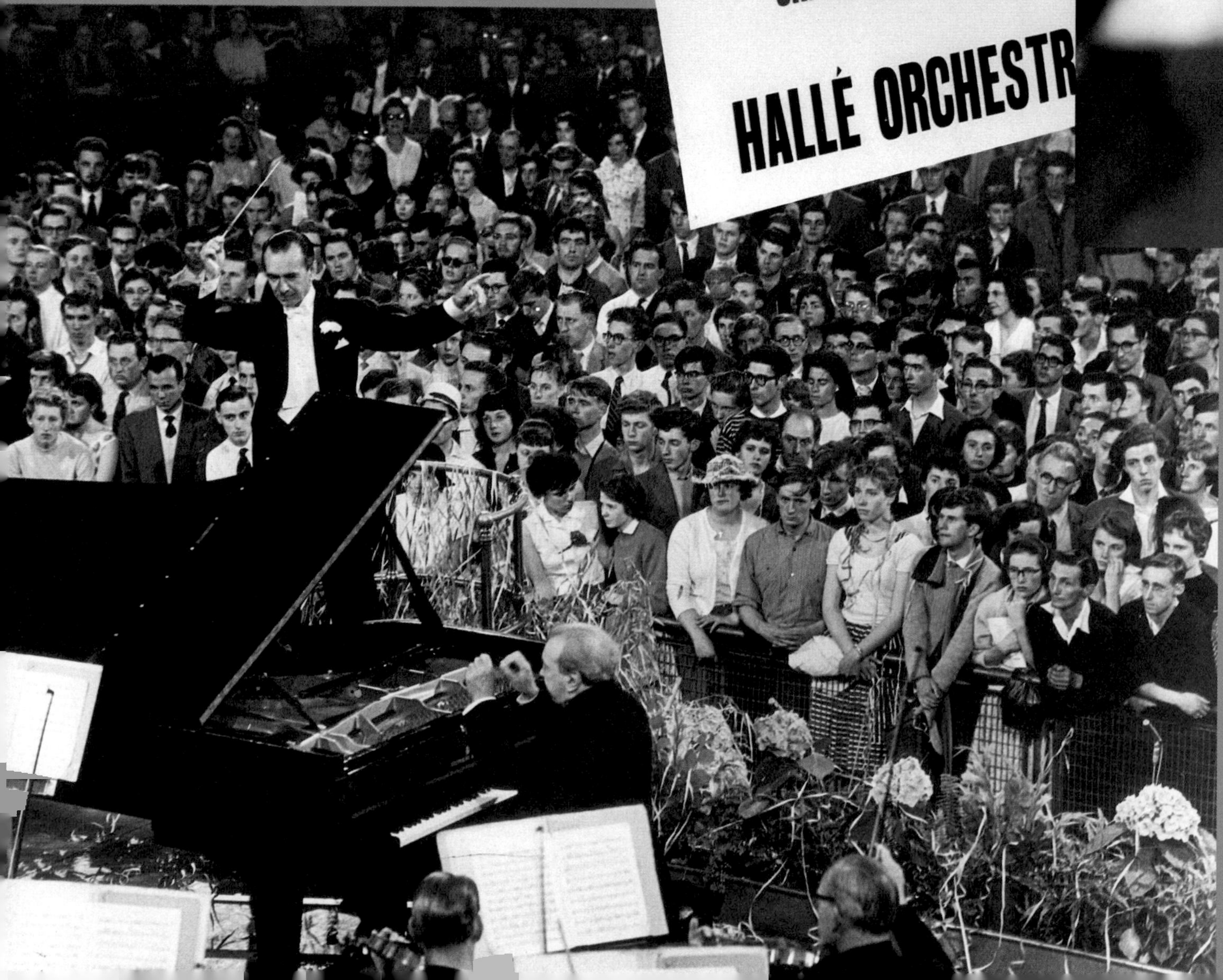

ROYAL ALBERT HALL
(Manager: C. S. Taylor)
HENRY WOOD
PROMENADE CONCERTS
59th SEASON 1953
SIR JOHN BARBIROLLI
HALLÉ ORCHESTR

Benno Moiseiwitsch is now one of the foremost of the world's pianists. He played to me this same year 1909 when he had just completed his studies under Leschetizky. I was deeply impressed and it was not long before [Robert] Newman had introduced him to the Promenade public. [...] I treasure the memory of a Saturday night dinner at the Savage Club in 1936 when 'Brother Benno' took the chair and introduced his great friend Rachmaninoff. I think every pianist of note in London must have been there that night.

Henry J. Wood, My Life of Music *(1938)*

Below: *Benno Moiseiwitsch plays the Rakhmaninov* Paganini Rhapsody *on the First Night of the 1958 season. Moiseiwitsch had made his Prom debut in 1914. His final season was in 1962. He performed in eighty-eight Proms*

GODFREY MACDOMNIC

BBC

Above: *Rehearsing for their first visit to the Proms in August 1953 are the Hallé and Barbirolli. Their concerts, and especially their Viennese Nights, were to become regular highlights*

Sir Adrian Boult rehearses the Royal Opera House Orchestra for their Prom on 21 July 1965

Vaughan Williams conducts the London Symphony Orchestra at the Proms in July 1946. The work is, aptly, his London Symphony

Below: *Speech-time. Sargent addresses his 'Beloved Promenaders' at the end of the 1952 season*

A televised performance of Vaughan Williams's Serenade to Music *under Sargent, given as part of the sixtieth-anniversary Prom in 1954. Ten of the original sixteen soloists from the 1938 premiere took part*

John Hollingsworth in 1951. He conducted the BBC
Symphony Orchestra, as well as the Royal Philharmonic
and the London Symphony, at many Proms between
1949 and 1959

Left: *Clifford Curzon
performs Beethoven's
'Emperor' Concerto with
Basil Cameron and the BBC
Symphony Orchestra on the
Last Night of the 1959
season. Curzon was revered
especially as a Mozart
player, and gave seventeen
performances of Mozart
concertos at the Proms*
GODFREY MACDOMNIC

Far left: *Clifford Curzon*
HULTON DEUTSCH

conductor when in 1921, aged twenty-six, he directed
his *An Impression on a Windy Day.* After the 1947 Prom
season the BBC declared that he was 'ideal in personality, showmanship and energy'. He was indeed popular
with audiences, but rather less so with orchestras and
the BBC, who often found him difficult to deal with.
Conservative in his tastes, he was happy to allow other
conductors to introduce new music. His particular speciality was the
performance of choral works. In the 1950s he introduced to the Proms
such large-scale pieces as Elgar's *Gerontius*, Verdi's *Requiem* and
Walton's *Belshazzar's Feast*, works which would have been impossible
to programme and rehearse in pre-war conditions.

Besides Sargent, a number of distinguished conductors left their
mark on the character of the Proms in these postwar years: there were
the Associate Conductors Stanford Robinson and John Hollingsworth;
the brilliant Constant Lambert, until his untimely death in 1951; Basil
Cameron, who conducted every year from 1941 until his retirement at
the age of eighty in 1964; and Adrian Boult, a perfectionist and cham-
pion of British composers, who retired as Principal Conductor of the
BBC SO in 1949, but appeared regularly at the Proms until 1977.

Towards the end of this period occurred the first appearances of
some conductors who were to figure largely in the future: Charles
Groves (1955); Colin Davis, Norman Del Mar, Alexander Gibson and
John Pritchard (all in 1960); Reginald Goodall and Charles Mackerras
(1961). In 1963 there was a sign of the Proms' widening horizons
when concerts were conducted by Georg Solti, Leopold Stokowski and
Carlo Maria Giulini.

*Sir Thomas Beecham
relaxing in the Artists' Room
at the Royal Albert Hall
on 15 September 1954 after
what was the second of his
three Prom appearances.
The first had been back
in 1915*

*14 September 1959. With
Sargent is soprano Heidi Krall.
The score is presumably
Strauss's* Four Last Songs,
*which they performed at the
Proms three nights later*

*Ever keen for new compositional challenges, Vaughan Williams
composed a Romance for Harmonica and Orchestra for Larry Adler,
given its London premiere at the Proms in September 1952*

*Here Adler (left) and VW relax after the performance. Above, Sargent
tries his hand*

Leopold Stokowski conducting at the Proms in his debut season in 1963 at the age of eighty-one. He was to return in 1964 and 1966

Above: *Stokowski rehearsing for the Proms at St Pancras Town Hall in July 1963. His grandson Richard Devitre listens*

Right: *Carlo Maria Giulini conducts Rossini's Stabat Mater on 23 August 1981. The great Italian conductor made his debut in 1963 and has returned on four occasions*

New Directions in the 1960s

*Sir William Glock,
BBC Controller, Music,
1959–72, at his final Press
Conference in 1973.
Glock had in fact made his
Prom debut as a pianist in
1940*

By the late 1950s, the Proms had come to be considered as solid and reliable as the Albert Hall itself. Every summer one could hear fine performances of the central classical repertoire, together with a certain amount of new or unusual music. But this very reliability had for some years been attracting criticism on two fronts. First, there was the view that perhaps the format of the Proms had become too easy to repeat, too predictable, too redolent of the committee that designed them. Secondly, that by faithfully concentrating on a 'central classical repertoire' – and who was to decide exactly what that should consist of? – there was a great deal of music, both old and new, that was not getting the airing it deserved. In short, the Proms were accused of containing too much repetition and too little adventure.

These, certainly, were the feelings of William Glock, who was appointed BBC Controller, Music, in 1959 and in the following year assumed personal responsibility for planning the Proms. He was anxious to bring Britain up to date with musical developments in continental Europe and the rest of the world, and to give Prom audiences the opportunity of experiencing as wide a range of music as possible. To accommodate this expansion of repertory, there had to be some loss of certain features that had become standard over the previous decades. To take a single example, one could no longer take for granted that all (or at least most) of the symphonies and concertos of Beethoven and Brahms would be heard in the course of a single season. On the other hand, it was rightly argued that these works, however great and central to our

*Pierre Boulez and Adrian
Boult at a rehearsal in 1972.
As Chief Conductor of the
BBC Symphony Orchestra from
1971–5, and Chief Guest
Conductor from 1975–7,
Boulez brought a wealth of
new music to the Proms.
He has returned regularly ever
since*

*Colin Davis directs BBC forces in a
performance of Beethoven's* Missa Solemnis
*at the start of the 1976 season.
The Prom was dedicated to the memory
of Rudolf Kempe, whose appointment as
Chief Conductor of the BBC Symphony
Orchestra had been cut short by his
early death*

*Of course there were new recruits to the Proms who were also to leave a powerful imprint;
and none more than Pierre Boulez, who first appeared at these concerts in 1965, and in the
three years from 1967 to 1969 gave historic concerts that are still vividly remembered. [...]
Boulez, like many others, must have been heartened by the rapt attention especially of the
young Promenaders, and by the warm response to programmes that were anything but
traditional. I think that quite often at these Boulez concerts there were many writers, artists,
and theatre people in the audience who came in search of some parallel to their own
contemporary experiences. There was an air sometimes of a more 'widespread' commitment
than usual to what was happening in the concert-hall; and that was exciting. [...] In asking
him to become in 1971 the next Chief Conductor of the BBC Symphony Orchestra, I was
influenced not only by the great performances he had often given, but also by my long
association with him, which, in one way and another, went back for nearly twenty years. I
admired him, too, as a composer, as a man of brilliance and imagination, and as a human
being.*

William Glock, Notes in Advance *(1991)*

The Piano Concerto was first performed at a Promenade Concert in the Queen's Hall on the 18th of August 1938, with Ben as soloist. We all went to hear the performance. During one energetic passage, one of his front studs (which he had borrowed from Kit because they were smarter than anything he had and he wanted to look his best for this important occasion) flew off and was never found again. There was quite a crowd outside the artists' entrance waiting for the pianist-composer to come out. It was the first time Benjamin had had so many admirers and so many requests for his autograph, and he was quite overcome.

Beth Britten, My Brother Benjamin (1986)

Benjamin Britten conducts Bach's St John Passion in July 1967. Britten attended Proms as a boy, and gave the premiere of his Piano Concerto in the 1938 season

To make music is wonderful. To make great music with a fine orchestra is very wonderful. To make great music with a fine orchestra to an audience which is at times so concentrated in its attention that it's almost frightening, and its appreciation is always overwhelming – to express this is wonderful beyond my words, but it's what I feel about it.

Malcolm Sargent,
Last Night speech,
15 September 1962

Left: *Constance Shacklock acknowledges applause on the Last Night of the 1961 Proms. She has sung Rule, Britannia! on more occasions than any other Last Night soloist*

54

Below: Pianist Daniel Barenboim discussing a point in Beethoven's Fourth Piano Concerto for a Prom performance on 31 August 1966 with Boulez. Barenboim has played on eight occasions, and conducted on six

Right: Malcolm Arnold preparing for a radio talk in 1966. His Cornish Dances had their London premiere during the Proms that year. All in all, his works have been heard twenty-three times at the Proms

musical life, could by now be heard from many other different sources. In the 1959 season there were twenty-six works which were new to the Proms. By 1964 the figure had risen to fifty-three; to fifty-eight in 1969 and sixty-seven in 1974.

The well-established pattern of the 1950s gave way over the next decade to a far more experimental style of programming, full of surprises, bold juxtapositions of style and period, thought-provoking mixtures of genre. Such programming was occasionally criticised for extravagance or for too great a concentration on novelty, but the criticisms could always be answered by pointing to the full houses and to the enthusiasm of the audiences.

With a widening of the repertory, there also came an enormous increase in the number of performers appearing at the Proms. From the early 1960s to the present day, we can follow a gradual transformation from a mainly British enterprise, not without innovations, but generally fairly conservative, to a major international festival. In their different ways, this new, wider identity of the Proms has been cultivated and refined by William Glock's successors, Robert Ponsonby (1973) and John Drummond (1986).

Boulez outside the Round House in 1974. This unconventional venue was used mostly for concerts of contemporary music. Boulez conducted there in 1971 and 1972

The cellist Jacqueline du Pré in 1961. She made her Prom debut in the Elgar concerto two years later. This famous interpretation was heard twice more at the Proms

Right: Isaac Stern, Eugene Istomin and Leonard Rose rehearsing Beethoven's Triple Concerto for a performance with Colin Davis and the BBC Symphony Orchestra on 5 September 1968

ALEX VON KOETTLITZ

Right: *Elgar Howarth conducting a programme of British brass band music on 7 September 1981*

Below: *A rehearsal of Ligeti's* Aventures *and* Nouvelle Aventures *at the Proms in 1984. Left to right are Penelope Walmsley-Clark, Omar Ebrahim and Linda Hirst*

MALCOLM CROWTHERS

Below: *Berlioz's rarely-heard* Grande Symphonie Funèbre et Triomphale *calls on the services of thirty-three clarinettists. Those assembled for the performance conducted by Sir John Pritchard on the First Night of the 1983 season included many of Britain's best-known players*

Below: *Emma Kirkby and members of the Taverner Consort, who performed the Florentine Intermedi of 1589 at the 1986 Proms*

Many innovations introduced during the 1960s have now become important regular features of each season, and while the overall style of the Proms continues (and must continue) to evolve, the variety of musical experience they offer remains constant. The Proms continue to be known as a mainly orchestral concert season, but in fact the orchestral repertory forms only one part – however major – of the enormously varied range of music offered today.

Operatic music was heard in the first Prom in 1895; but opera in general is now heard in a very different way, with an 'all or nothing' approach. Short extracts have become exceptional, while concert (or semi-staged) performances of entire operas are now among the greatest attractions of modern seasons. In 1961, Glyndebourne Opera brought its *Don Giovanni* to the Proms, followed by *Così fan tutte* and *The Marriage of Figaro* in 1962 and 1963. These were the first complete full-length opera performances at the Proms, and established a double tradition: the annual visit from Glyndebourne, and performances by other companies or by the BBC's own forces of works which Prom audiences might never have the opportunity to see in the theatre: Schoenberg's *Moses and Aaron*, for example (1965), or Berlioz's *Benvenuto Cellini* (1972). A particularly memorable occasion was the Glyndebourne visit of 1982, when Janet Baker made her farewell to the operatic stage in the role of Gluck's Orfeo. (Her final appearance at the Proms was on the First Night of the 1984 season, singing Elgar's *Sea Pictures*).

A performance of the

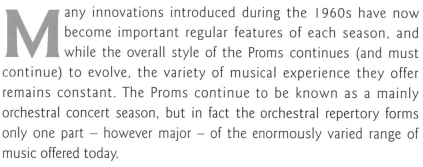

A member of the group Nexus blows into a conch shell in John Cage's Third Construction *in the 1984 season*

Below: *Dame Janet Baker (Orpheus) rehearses with members of the Glyndebourne Chorus for the performance of Gluck's* Orfeo ed Euridice *on 11 August 1982 which marked her official farewell to opera. The great mezzo-soprano's thirty-five appearances at the Proms between 1960 and 1984 included some of the most memorable of recent times*

It must have been after a visit to the Glyndebourne Opera in the summer of 1960 that it suddenly occurred to me that, by inviting the company at the end of their next season to come up to London and give a performance of Don Giovanni *that had been rehearsed to the last degree, the Prom audience would be offered an example of opera at its best. I think I had imagined only a concert performance; but Moran Caplat and some of his colleagues at Glyndebourne suggested that if it were semi-staged the impact would be far greater. It was a brilliant idea. The performance when it came on 21 August was a quite wonderful experience. The singing seemed to flower more generously than in the rather boxy acoustics of Glyndebourne itself, and I think many must have felt that the intense and creative attention of the Promenaders to every phrase and action contributed greatly to the general inspiration. Opera had come to the Proms to stay.*

William Glock, Notes in Advance *(1991)*

Javanese dancers (below) and members of the Sasono Mulio Gamelan Orchestra of Surakarta (left) in a 1979 Prom

ALEX VON KOETTLITZ

ALEX VON KOETTLITZ

An all-night concert of Indian Music devised by Vilayat Khan was one of the innovations of the 1981 season. Among India's most distinguished musical families, members of the Khan dynasty appeared in 1971 and 1978, and returned again in 1989 and 1994

(Back, left to right) William Mathias, Colin Matthews, Brian Elias, (front) Sir Michael Tippett and Robert Saxton, with the bust of Henry Wood in 1984. All five composers had premieres that season

complete Third Act of *Götterdämmerung* in 1963 established a different sort of 'Wagner Night', far removed from anything that Henry Wood could have envisaged. Over the next few years there were whole acts from *Die Walküre*, *Parsifal*, *Tristan* and *Siegfried* and, over two evenings in 1972, a complete performance of *Parsifal*.

Henry Wood's performance of Monteverdi's *Sonata sopra Sancta Maria* in 1922 was far in advance of its time (what we would not give for a recording of it!). Even in 1969, nearly half a century later, a concert of music from the fourteenth and fifteenth centuries was still considered quite a novelty, particularly in the Albert Hall. Since then, however, performances of early music have become important features of every season. As well as delving backwards in time to the Middle Ages, the Proms have reflected the modern interest in historical performing styles which has had such changing influences on our perception of music from the Baroque and Classical periods.

In recent decades the Proms have tried to incorporate something of the universality of musical experience by presenting concerts of music from beyond the European tradition. In 1971 Imrat Khan performed two Indian ragas during a late-night Prom. Since then, Indian music has been heard regularly, and the Proms have offered performances by ensembles from several other different cultures, including Indonesia, Thailand, Korea and Japan.

Other Prom events of recent years which have gone well beyond the 'traditional' repertory have included brass band and steel band performances (linked with a picnic in Kensington Gardens); children's Proms; one by the Merce Cunningham Dance Company;

Elisabeth Lutyens with conductor Ronald Zollman after the world premiere of her Fleur du Silence at the Round House on 2 August 1981. This was the last of her six Prom premieres, the first being in 1940

I think I conducted at the Proms for the first time in 1953. Malcolm Sargent, my old conducting teacher from Royal College days, had been a bit naughty and had refused to direct the premiere of my Corelli Fantasia at the Edinburgh Festival that year. He said it was 'too intellectual'. So I took over that performance and the repeat at the Proms. Unfortunately, one of the two string orchestras involved got a bar out in the fugue section. I didn't know who was supposed to be playing where, so I sang out a rehearsal number and eventually things came right again. Sargent ticked off the players afterwards.

Sir Michael Tippett (1980), quoted in 'Quote Proms Unquote', compiled by David Cox, BBC Proms Guide 1990

Right: *Sir Michael Tippett acknowledges applause after the first European performance of* The Mask of Time *(23 July 1984). Behind him are soloists Faye Robinson, Felicity Palmer and John Cheek, as well as conductor Andrew Davis and chorus-master Brian Wright*

Left: *The Italian composer Luigi Nono conducting the London premiere of his cantata* Sul ponte di Hiroshima *on 10 September 1963*

Outside the Royal Albert Hall pianist Charles Rosen (left) and composer Elliott Carter look at the score of Carter's Piano Concerto, which Rosen played in September 1980

Dominic Muldowney (left) and Peter Donohoe rehearsing Muldowney's Piano Concerto, a BBC commission which received its first performance on 27 July 1983

Right (left to right): *Sir John Pritchard, Harrison Birtwistle and Malcolm Binns, in a rehearsal break between Birtwistle's* The Triumph of Time *and Mendelssohn's Second Piano Concerto, 16 August 1982*

Jonathan Harvey acknowledges the applause of the BBC SO and conductor Sir Charles Groves after a performance of Persephone Dream on 1 September 1981

9 September 1982: Richard Rodney Bennett after a rehearsal of Anniversaries, commissioned by the BBC, which received its world premiere that evening

Oliver Knussen rehearsing his Second Symphony on 24 August 1984. Several of his works have received their premieres at the Proms.

ALEX VON KOETTLITZ

Witold Lutosławski (left) and Heinz
Holliger at a rehearsal of Lutosławski's
Double Concerto for oboe, harp and
chamber orchestra (1981). The harpist
was Holliger's wife, Ursula

ALEX VON KOETTLITZ

and jazz of various shades performed by the National Youth Jazz
Orchestra, Loose Tubes and the Wynton Marsalis Band.

New music at the Proms reflects new music around the world; but
starting in 1961 a special feature of each season has been the com-
missioning of new works by the BBC specifically for performance at
the Proms. Dozens of British composers owe their reputations to this
practice, and a Prom commission is a much sought-after prize, for it
guarantees a well-prepared performance in front of the most receptive
audience a composer could wish for. This is equally true, of course, for
composers whose music may be receiving a first British or London
performance.

Oliver Knussen and
Robert Saxton at a rehearsal
of Saxton's The Ring of
Eternity, a 1983 Prom
premiere

*[The Promenaders are] young, keen, enthusiastic, as if they were going to a
football match. In type they're exactly the same as in my young days. The only
differences are their wider knowledge of music and their greater curiosity about
things they haven't heard before. [...] The youngsters have got used to hearing
serious things and out-of-the-way things. It's fascinating to see how willing
they are to give a fair hearing to experimental stuff. We saw that last year with
the electronic music [Berio's* Perspectives, *8 August 1960], although there was
a certain amount of grinning. They are less readily shocked than youngsters
used to be. They are willing to accept anything. Of course, we must be careful
not to give them anything that is not worth listening to.*

Malcolm Sargent, quoted in Charles Reid, Malcolm Sargent: a biography *(1968)*

Below: *The composer Giles Swayne (with his son
Orlando) and conductor John Poole (left), discussing
his score of CRY at a rehearsal for the Prom
performance in August 1983*

MALCOLM CROWTHERS

Below: *Rehearsal for the world premiere of
Colin Matthews's Cello Concerto, 10 September
1984: conductor David Atherton (left) with
the composer, and soloist
Alexander Baillie*

MALCOLM CROWTHERS

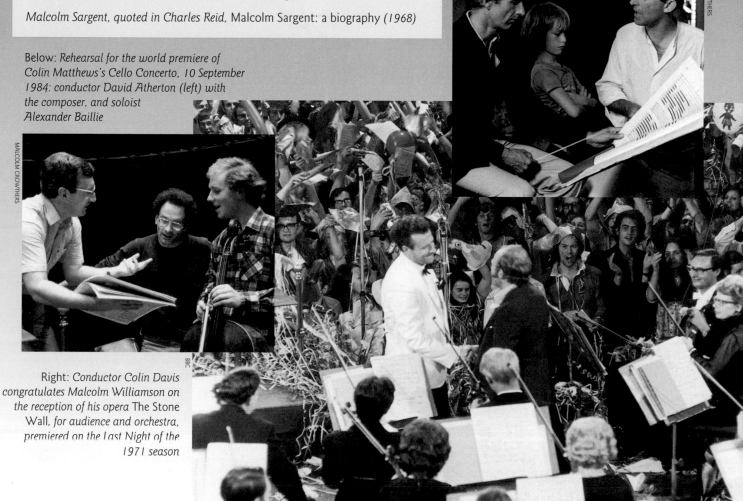

BBC

Right: *Conductor Colin Davis
congratulates Malcolm Williamson on
the reception of his opera* The Stone
Wall, *for audience and orchestra,
premiered on the Last Night of the
1971 season*

The first visit by a foreign orchestra to the Proms:
Gennady Rozhdestvensky and the Moscow Radio Orchestra
are hailed by the Proms audience in August 1966.
Later, as Chief Conductor of the BBC SO between 1978 and
1981, Rozhdestvensky would become a familiar and much
loved figure at the Proms

Right: Lucia Popp is the soprano soloist in this rehearsal of
the Brahms Requiem with the London Philharmonic
Orchestra conducted by Klaus Tennstedt in the 1984 season.
Thomas Allen sang the baritone solo

ДОБРО
ПОЖАЛОВАТЬ
ГЕНАДИЙ

Sir Georg Solti and the Chicago Symphony Orchestra gave two performances in the 1981 season

MORE PERFORMERS

In 1966 the Moscow Radio Orchestra, conducted by Gennady Rozhdestvensky (later to become Chief Conductor of the BBC SO), became the first of many foreign orchestras to play at the Proms. Over the next three years there were visits by the Amsterdam Concertgebouw Orchestra, the Polish Radio Symphony Orchestra, the USSR State Philharmonic and the Czech Philharmonic. The list has continued to grow up to the present: although today the mainstay of the Proms is still provided by the various BBC orchestras, a modern season will be performed by literally dozens of other orchestras and ensembles from Britain and from all over the world – there were nineteen in 1976 and twenty-four in 1986. Proms have been given by all the major European orchestras, including the Berlin and Vienna philharmonics, and by several American orchestras, including the 'big five' from New York, Chicago, Boston, Cleveland and Philadelphia. As well as international symphony orchestras, the Proms have hosted a number of smaller chamber orchestras and ensembles. The list of conductors who made Prom debuts from the mid-1960s onwards is quite simply an international directory: in order of first appearances, one could begin the list with Bernard Haitink, Claudio Abbado, Evgeny Svetlanov, Christoph von Dohnányi, Eliahu Inbal, Lorin Maazel, André Previn, Erich Leinsdorf ...

Simon Rattle first conducted at the Proms in 1976, and in 1985 Vladimir Ashkenazy, who had performed regularly as a pianist since 1964, appeared for the first time as a conductor.

As with orchestras and conductors, so with the list of world-famous soloists who have performed at the Proms over the last thirty years. This too is nothing less than a directory of the great musicians of our time – not that they were necessarily well-known when they first appeared at the Proms, which are famous for including as yet unknown talents alongside the world's biggest names. It is important to remember, though, that the Proms do not operate on a star system: whatever is included in the programmes always has to justify its presence on purely musical merits.

Günter Wand rehearsing a programme of Mozart and Brahms with the BBC SO in 1983. Over the years his performances with the orchestra of the Austro-German repertory, and Bruckner in particular, have become legendary

Conductor André Previn has made seven appearances at the Proms. The most memorable was in 1974, when Thomas Allen, the baritone soloist in Orff's Carmina Burana, *fainted, and was replaced by a member of the audience*

Below: *A masterly exponent of the Russian repertory, Kirill Kondrashin included Prokofiev and Rakhmaninov in his programme with the Amsterdam Concertgebouw Orchestra in 1980. Here he rehearses for his single appearance at the Proms (he died the following year)*

Left: Jorge Bolet played the virtuoso repertoire with inimitable panache. He appeared on three occasions at the Proms between 1982 and 1988. This photograph shows him in 1982, when he performed Liszt's First Concerto, and his Funérailles in memory of Clifford Curzon, who had died the previous day

ALEX VON KOETTLITZ

MALCOLM CROWTHERS

ALEX VON KOETTLITZ

Above: Elisabeth Leonskaja is the soloist in this 1983 rehearsal of Tchaikovsky's First Concerto with the BBC Philharmonic Orchestra under its Principal Conductor Edward Downes

One of the last heirs of the Romantic tradition of pianism, Shura Cherkassky rehearses Chopin's Second Concerto with Richard Hickox at the Proms in 1983. Since his first appearance in 1955, Cherkassky has appeared on twelve occasions

Right: Brahms's First Piano Concerto performed by Alfred Brendel with Sir Charles Groves and the BBC SO in 1981. In addition to concertos by Mozart, Beethoven, Brahms and Schoenberg, Brendel has played two of Beethoven's sonatas and the Diabelli Variations

ALEX VON KOETTLITZ

ALEX VON KOETTLITZ

Left: Yo-Yo Ma is the soloist in a performance of Dvořák's Cello Concerto in 1983 with the Royal Philharmonic Orchestra under Sir Charles Groves. Between 1955 and 1989 Sir Charles made more than fifty appearances at the Proms

Chamber music at the Proms: György Pauk (violin), Ralph Kirshbaum (cello) and Peter Frankl (piano) perform Schubert's B flat Piano Trio in 1981

MALCOLM CROWTHERS

Leading Mozart interpreter Alicia de Larrocha plays the Concerto K488 with Yuri Temirkanov and the Royal Philharmonic Orchestra in August 1984

Pianists Imogen Cooper and
Anne Queffélec played concertos for
two pianos by Poulenc in 1982 and
Mozart in 1984. As individual
soloists Cooper has played on
thirteen occasions, Queffélec on one

Wagnerian diva Birgit Nilsson sang songs
by Strauss and excerpts from operas by
Strauss and Wagner in the 1981 season.
Her previous appearance at the Proms
consisted of Isolde's Liebestod, and
Brünnhilde in Act 3 of
Götterdämmerung, under Solti in 1963

Maurizio Pollini takes a bow after his performance
of Mozart's Piano Concerto K491 with Simon Rattle
and the CBSO in 1993

Right: *Sir John Pritchard conducts Mozart's edition of Handel's Messiah on the opening night of the 1985 season. As Chief Conductor of the BBC SO from 1982 until 1989, Pritchard interpreted a wide repertoire at the Proms, receiving particular acclaim in late-Romantic music*

Jane Glover first conducted at the Proms in 1985 and has appeared on six occasions since

Below: *Roger Norrington conducts a programme of Beethoven and Schubert in 1989. Norrington is one of a generation of British conductors to bring historically informed performance practice to the Proms*

Above: *Krzysztof Penderecki conducts a rehearsal of his* St Luke Passion *in 1983*

Left: *29 August 1984: Sir Charles Mackerras, Chief Guest Conductor of the Australian Youth Orchestra, brings the musicians to their feet at the end of the last concert of their first European tour*

Above: *Bernard Haitink rehearses the Amsterdam Concertgebouw Orchestra for their Prom appearances in September 1970. Haitink conducted his first Prom in 1966, a debut followed by fifty-seven further concerts to date*

Right: *Gennady Rozhdestvensky and the BBC SO on the 1979 First Night*

Below: *The great German conductor Rudolf Kempe directs the BBC SO in a programme of Prokofiev, Liszt and Dvořák on 29 August 1975, the last of his eleven Prom appearances*

Below: *John Eliot Gardiner, who made his Prom debut in 1968 conducting his own Monteverdi Choir in Monteverdi's* Vespers. *In twenty-eight subsequent appearances with a variety of groups he has shed new light on a wide range of repertory*

MALCOLM CROWTHERS

ALEX VON KOETTLITZ

MALCOLM CROWTHERS

Joshua Bell rehearsing Tchaikovsky's Violin Concerto with the BBC SO under its Principal Guest Conductor Alexander Lazarev in the 1994 season's 'Tchaikovsky Night'

The line-up of soloists for Rossini's Stabat Mater under Giulini in 1981: Dalmacio Gonzalez, Katia Ricciarelli, Lucia Valentini-Terrani and Ruggero Raimondi

Above: St Paul's Church, Knightsbridge, was a venue used for small-scale events from 1986 to 1989. Here, Anthony Rooley and The Consort of Musicke (with Emma Kirkby, far left), rehearse a programme of 'Songs for Prince Henry', July 1987

Kensington Town Hall, where several late-night Proms were given during the 1988 and 1989 seasons. The Australian new music group Flederman takes a bow, July 1988

CONCERTS TODAY

he basic outline of a Prom season has in some other respects changed very little in a century. A typical eight-week season will run from the middle of July to the middle of September, with concerts every day, including Sunday. In 1968 the Proms opened not on the traditional Saturday but on Friday, with a special concert of English music dedicated to the memory of Malcolm Sargent, who had died the previous year. Since then it has been standard to open the Proms on a Friday, usually with a big choral work.

Concerts tend to be shorter than they were in the past. Henry Wood's programmes seem very long now, but even in the 1950s certain Proms might consist of two major concertos and two major symphonies – something that modern audiences would probably find rather indigestible and orchestras would be reluctant to rehearse. Today's more concentrated programmes generally last from 7.30 to 9.30, including a twenty-minute interval. Occasionally, programmes featuring difficult or challenging works might be split up into three parts, rather than two.

Conductor Esa-Pekka Salonen and cellist Heinrich Schiff discuss a point during a rehearsal of Shostakovich's First Cello Concerto with the Swedish Radio Symphony Orchestra in the 1990 season

A welcome innovation of the 1970s was the introduction of a number of extra late-night Proms after the evening's main event. These late concerts, usually featuring small forces or more intimate styles of music, have become a regular feature. From the same period came the institution of Pre-Prom Talks, which

Opera at the Proms: Tchaikovsky's The Queen of Spades, *acclaimed at Glyndebourne earlier in the year, receives a semi-staged performance in the 1992 season. Glyndebourne's first visit to the Proms was in 1961, and the company has returned almost every season since*

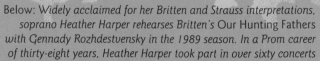

Below: Widely acclaimed for her Britten and Strauss interpretations, soprano Heather Harper rehearses Britten's Our Hunting Fathers with Gennady Rozhdestvensky in the 1989 season. In a Prom career of thirty-eight years, Heather Harper took part in over sixty concerts

The first woman to conduct a complete Prom, Odaline de la Martinez, made her debut in 1984 and has appeared on four occasions since, the most notable being her revival of Smyth's The Wreckers in 1994

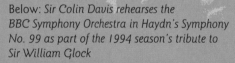

Below: Sir Colin Davis rehearses the BBC Symphony Orchestra in Haydn's Symphony No. 99 as part of the 1994 season's tribute to Sir William Glock

Left: *Conductor David Atherton accompanies harpist Sidonie Goossens from the stage after the fiftieth-anniversary performance of Vaughan Williams's* Serenade to Music *in 1988. The eighty-nine-year-old harpist, a member of one of Britain's most eminent musical families, had played in the first performance in 1938. Her first solo credit at the Proms had been eight years before that. David Atherton has appeared on forty-one occasions at the Proms, the first in 1968 when, at the age of twenty-four, he was the youngest ever conductor*

have proved a useful means of introducing some of the new music being played each season.

Starting in 1971 there were experiments with different venues for some concerts. The Royal Opera House hosted a Prom performance of Musorgsky's *Boris Godunov*; Beethoven's *Missa Solemnis* was performed in Westminster Cathedral, and the Round House in Chalk Farm was employed for a late-night concert. Since 1990, however, all concerts have been held in the Albert Hall — it is, after all, able to accommodate larger audiences, and even the smaller numbers who attend the late-night concerts have found that a surprisingly intimate atmosphere can be created if the lighting is skilfully employed.

A few statistics might give some idea of the variety available at the Proms today. A quick glance over the past ten years shows the following averages: each season of sixty-two concerts features thirty-two orchestras or ensembles performing under forty-six conductors. There is music by eighty-nine composers, twenty-five of whom are living.

The hundredth season in 1994 consisted of sixty-eight concerts, featuring thirty-five different orchestras and ensembles, eighteen choirs, fifty conductors, forty-two instrumental soloists and ninety-five solo singers. The music performed was by 118 different composers.

After a 1972 performance of the Elgar Violin Concerto, Yehudi Menuhin joins hands with Sir Adrian Boult. Menuhin first played at the Proms in 1946, and has made thirteen appearances in all, including one as a conductor

Violinist Nigel Kennedy, who has played concertos by Brahms, Tchaikovsky, Dvořák and Walton at the Proms. His debut was in 1981

The Protecting Veil, *John Tavener's work for cello and strings, went on to win enormous popularity after its Prom premiere on 4 September 1989. Earlier that day, composer (right) and soloist Steven Isserlis seem to sense their success*

Hungarian soloists Julia Hamari and Laszlo Polgar perform Bartók's Duke Bluebeard's Castle *under Hungarian conductor Peter Eötvös in the 1984 season. As a Principal Guest Conductor of the BBC SO from 1985 to 1988, Eötvös's Prom appearances concentrated on contemporary music. One of his own works is scheduled for the 1995 season*

c1960

Last Night of the Proms queue, 1949

72

TOPHAM

1941

AUDIENCES: A VIEW FROM THE ARENA

The Proms were founded in order to fulfil Robert Newman's ambition of 'training the public by easy stages'. We have seen how he and Wood succeeded in creating their audience a hundred years ago. What about the modern descendants of that 'public for classical and modern music'?

BBC interviewer Frank Phillips talks to Arena Promenaders in 1942

Perhaps the most striking fact of all about the Prom audiences is their size. Concert life inevitably tends to suffer in a harsh economic climate, but over the past decade the Proms have regularly achieved attendance figures of over eighty per cent.

If you buy a ticket for one of the seats in the Albert Hall – whether in the stalls, the boxes or the balcony – you will realise long before the players come onto the stage what makes the Proms so special and different from other concerts: the Arena in front of you is crowded with people, many of them very young, who have come to stand through the concert. Several have bought season tickets, guaranteeing entrance to all the concerts for much less than £2.00. Others may have queued for hours to get in, for places cannot be reserved. In addition to the Prommers in the Arena, there are also several hundred (almost invisible from below) standing high up in the Gallery.

For many of these people, the Proms have become a social as well as a musical occasion. Modern Prom-goers may not eat, smoke or drink (not, at least, during the concerts), but this abstinence doesn't inhibit the general informality, or the development of various other social activities in and around the Albert Hall.

Over the years, many foreign musicians have expressed their astonishment at the concentration of Prom audiences, who can stand in perfect silence throughout the longest works.

Commentators on the Proms audience overlook the psychological effect of standing. By standing, the listener's concentrative powers are increased and his tendency to mentally wander and to adopt the usual irritating mannerisms [...] diminished. There is no doubt, too, that the strain of standing in order to listen is tremendous and directly contributes to the uncontrolled desire to join in the mass emotion of clapping, stamping, and generally releasing a tension which has been growing throughout a work. Such emotion is heightened by the music, and when a soloist of international repute is interpreting it, the noisy approbations become a delirious frenzy comparable with the exhibitionism of Jitterbugging, Buchmanism, and All-in Wrestling. It will not do for an audience which has come to worship at the Shrine of St Cecilia thus to demean itself, and this behaviour must stop. During this last summer season [1946] the applause given to Menuhin after he had played the Elgar Violin Concerto amounted to nothing less than hysteria. To have demanded his presence seven or eight times must have been as trying for him as it was intolerable for those of the audience who had gone to hear Elgar performed, not just to see the violinist.

'Audience of the Proms', George Dannatt, in Penguin Music Magazine No. 2, ed. Ralph Hill (1947)

Last Night queue, 1947

*11 July 1943: the first-ever Sunday Prom.
Sir Henry watches from a box*

Sir Henry Wood leads the audience in Rule, Britannia! on the Last Night of the 1942 season

Right: *Promenaders
adorn Sir Malcolm with
a wreath of flowers on
the Last Night of the
1952 season*

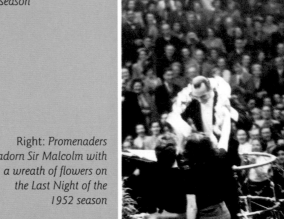

Up in the Gallery on the Last Night of the 1961 season

The Hall viewed from a box

Above: A rapt Albert Hall listens
to the Nash Ensemble playing
Mozart's Wind Serenade in C minor,
26 August 1984

In the Gallery, 16 September 1961

c1960

Below: *Around the fountain*

Too often have I heard and read that the 'Promenader' is 'uncritical', 'fanatical', 'hysterical', 'uneducated musically', 'lacking in discrimination' ... But one can judge affection, love, in other people, only by seeing how much they are willing to suffer or deny themselves in favour of that which they adore – and I have seen hundreds of people 'queueing' for hours; then standing for hours at a concert; then shouting and cheering their acclamations, refreshed in body and spirit by the excitement of the art of music. They have given much of their patience and endurance, and have received the more in return. [...]

All soloists love performing at a 'Prom'. They are assured of the welcome of friendship; a silent hearing which receives music and gives back inspiration; and, at the end, they are refreshed by an acclamation which makes them feel their efforts were not entirely in vain, and spurs them on to a more perfect achievement.

Malcolm Sargent, Introduction to The Story of the Proms *(1955)*

Richard Baker talks to the viewers at home

This intensity is much appreciated by performers, who sense an immediate communication, often hard to achieve in other large halls.

This rapt concentration applies only during the music, however: before and after, the Prommers are less quiet. Robert Simpson once expressed the wish that they would eventually discover that 'the silence after the last note is part of the music'. One sometimes hears complaints that they are undiscriminating in their applause. This is forgivable. A Prom audience is not made up of professional musicians or critics, and many of the younger Prommers may be hearing one of the great masterpieces for the first time – an experience that older and more critical listeners can only envy.

Sir Michael Tippett applauds

The Prommers become the centre of attention on the Last Night, a noisy, ritualistic affair whose second part follows a well-established format with audience participation in such party-pieces as Henry Wood's *Fantasia on British Sea-Songs*, first devised for the Trafalgar Centenary in 1905. *Rule, Britannia!* and Parry's *Jerusalem* strike a nationalistic note rarely heard in other circumstances nowadays.

The Last Night has for many years been the source of an annual controversy. As early as 1950 the BBC wondered whether Sargent and his audience had got out of control: 'Sir Malcolm, however, is prepared to encourage audience enthusiasm to the maximum point at which he can restrain it, and although [we] feel that the point was perhaps reached and even passed this year, I do not know that Sir Malcolm would agree'. For his part, Sargent is reported as saying that 'if people can get as enthusiastic about music as they do about football, that is all to the good'.

A distinguished chronicler of musical events, the artist Milein Cosman drew this sketch in the Gallery of the Royal Albert Hall

Opinions about the Last Night of the Proms are sharply divided. To some it is a detestable occasion, an out-of-place and out-of-date expression of jingoism; others staunchly maintain that it is a perfectly innocent celebration of music-making, and an entirely appropriate way of celebrating the end of the season. Whatever the merits of either argument, the Prommers themselves have ferociously resisted any attempts to change the format of the Last Night. And of course it *is* only the last night, utterly untypical of the sixty-or-so evenings that have preceded it.

Promenaders from Portsmouth breakfasting before the Last Night in 1965

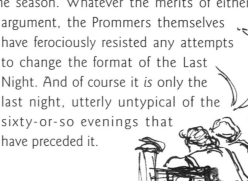

Left: On the Last Night of the 1942 Proms, Freddie Grisewood interviews the three conductors taking part in the concert:
(left to right) Basil Cameron, Sir Henry Wood and Sir Adrian Boult

Below: Grisewood talks to four members of the BBC SO:
(left to right) Nick Chesterman (double bass), Sidonie Goossens (harp), Aubrey Brain (horn) and Paul Beard (leader)

[The BBC took over the Proms in 1927.] This meant that if the shortcomings due to hurriedly prepared programmes were not to become too obvious (for much that is missed in the concert hall can be discerned on the wireless) more rehearsal time had to be allowed. Sir Henry often told the orchestra: 'It won't do, you know, it won't do. Millions of people are listening to this performance, and they've all got the score with them. And all the children who are taught music in the schools are listening in, the little beasts. And they'll say, "It's not in tune, Daddy, it's not in tune!"'

Thomas Russell, The Proms (1949)

BROADCASTING THE PROMS

When the BBC took over responsibility for the Proms in 1927, it was able to provide financial stability and reliable organisation. The most far-reaching effect, however, was that with the advent of broadcasting the Proms could be heard by vastly greater audiences. Rather than discouraging people from going to concerts, as some feared at the time, broadcasting actually seems to have had the reverse effect – by bringing the Proms to wider atten-

tion, broadcasting functioned as a new means of publicity and helped attract many more people to live concert-going. For those who would never be able to get to the Queen's Hall, it was often a revelation. Frederick Delius, lying blind and paralysed in France, was able to hear his *Song of the High Hills* on the wireless in 1932 and immediately sent a telegram: 'Thanks, dear Wood, for your lovely interpretation ...'.

A cameraman focuses on the Promenaders as Sir Malcolm Sargent conducts them in Rule, Britannia! *in 1965*

At first, only Part One of each concert – the most substantial part – was relayed from the Queen's Hall, but by 1947 virtually every note performed at the Proms was being broadcast live from the Albert Hall. Concerts were divided between the BBC Light Programme, the Home Service and the new Third Programme. The Last Night of the Proms was televised for the first time in 1947, and the First Night in 1953. Since the mid-1960s, all the Proms have been broadcast in stereo, around ten concerts every season are televised, and about half are broadcast by the BBC World Service. BBC Radio International (formerly BBC Transcription) will send recordings from the Proms to forty-five countries around the world. Since the 1970s the Proms have formed

Below: Acoustic technicians and bassoonist Colin Beak perform tests in the Albert Hall prior to the raising of the 'flying saucers'

Left and above: *A television relay may use as many as six or seven cameras, carefully positioned to give the widest range of attractive and informative images*

Below left: *In the outside broadcast vans images from the cameras in the hall are selected for transmission*

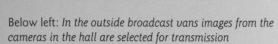

A production assistant, a director and a vision mixer monitor each camera's pictures and select the shot to be transmitted according to a planned camera script

BROADCASTING PHOTOS: ALEX VON KOETTLITZ

Left: *An outside broadcast sound supervisor checks the distribution chains to the BBC World Service, BBC Television and BBC Radio International*

Below: *A studio manager balances the sound at the main mixing console in the control room*

The announcer's contribution and any pre-recorded interviews are added in

It is difficult to describe the main impulses that lay behind the transformation that took place during those fourteen years at the Proms. I certainly set out with many individual works that I wanted passionately to include, and was aware, for example, of a hundred outstanding pieces by Mozart that had never yet been heard at these concerts. But with many strands of earlier music, and with contemporary works too, the choices I made depended on a process of self-education, helped by a strain of curiosity that I think never left me; and then – perhaps as a schoolmaster's son – by a strong impulse to try and pass on whatever had aroused my enthusiasm and admiration. [...]

Of course I never forgot that I had the great blessing of a spirit of enterprise that had been established at the Proms for half a century by Sir Henry Wood. Nor did my successors, Robert Ponsonby and John Drummond. Since 1974 they have preserved this enterprise, while adapting the programmes and performances to an ever-changing musical climate.

William Glock, Notes in Advance *(1991)*

the major part of Radio 3's live summer programming, and several Proms are given repeat broadcasts at other times of the year.

A capacity audience in the Albert Hall may consist of well over 5,000 people – an enormous number compared to most concert halls. Yet this is only a very small fraction of the total audience for the Proms. Nowhere else in the world are over sixty concerts broadcast live on consecutive nights and followed so closely by listeners. Estimates for the total audience in recent seasons – in the hall, and for radio and television – have been around forty million.

The BBC's justified reputation for technical excellence is based on the high professional skills, and often years of experience, of everybody involved. Broadcasting the Proms is a complex operation, often requiring as much detailed rehearsal as the music itself. Those most in the public eye (or ear, rather) are the announcers, who as well as introducing the players and the music have to convey something of the atmosphere in the hall, and must be prepared at a moment's notice to explain any emergencies that might crop up. Unheard by the public are the dozens of technical staff, each with a particular specialisation. The number and placing of the microphones will probably be different for each concert, depending on the type of music being performed, the forces involved and the balance between the performers. When the concert is to be televised, the appropriate lighting has to be arranged, the cameras placed strategically, and the shots and angles carefully planned in advance.

ALEX VON KOETTLITZ

Three Controllers: (left to right) Sir William Glock, John Drummond and Robert Ponsonby. Between them they have planned thirty-six Prom seasons

Liz Russell of the Proms unit sorts out a problem at rehearsal

Susan Sharpe, Radio 3 announcer for the evening

Andrew Davis and the BBC SO in the foyer of the Royal Albert Hall, 1993

JACQUELINE WYATT

ALEX VON KOETTLITZ

THE BBC ORCHESTRAS

The planning, organisation, presentation and broadcasting of the Proms demonstrate the BBC's role as the most important patron of music in the country – a vital role in a land where government support of the arts in general and music in particular has never been noted for its generosity.

A major effect of this patronage is the contribution of the BBC's own orchestras. Around fifteen Proms each season are given by the London-based BBC Symphony Orchestra. A further fifteen concerts will be divided between the BBC Philharmonic, based in Manchester, the BBC Scottish Symphony Orchestra, the BBC National Orchestra of Wales and the BBC Concert Orchestra. In addition, there are important contributions from the BBC Singers and the BBC Symphony Chorus.

The BBC Symphony Orchestra, founded in 1930 as a direct descendant of Henry Wood's Queen's Hall Orchestra, soon reached a very high level of achievement under its first principal conductor, Adrian Boult. Arturo Toscanini declared in 1939 that he had never conducted a finer orchestra. Boult was succeeded by Malcolm Sargent, who was then followed by Rudolf Schwarz (1957) and Antal Dorati (1959). The BBC SO's Chief Conductor will always, of course, be a figure of great importance at the Proms. From 1967 the post was held by Colin Davis, who is associated by many listeners with the outstanding performances he gave (and continues to give) of music by Mozart, Beethoven, Berlioz, Tippett and Stravinsky. Very different in both style and musical character is his successor Pierre Boulez, a firm ally of

A Prom in 1989. Andrew Davis has achieved an extraordinary rapport with Proms audiences since his debut in 1971. His sixty-nine appearances have included five memorable Last Nights

CLIVE BARDA/PERFORMING ARTS LIBRARY

BBC

Last Night, 1989

Andrew Davis and Sir John Pritchard share a joke at the Press Conference announcing Davis's appointment as Chief Conductor of the BBC SO in succession to Sir John from 1989

The BBC Philharmonic with its Principal Conductor Yan Pascal Tortelier at Manchester's Free Trade Hall in 1992. The orchestra regularly gives four concerts each season

Below: *Lorin Maazel conducting the BBC SO and vast choral forces on the First Night of the 1986 Proms in Mahler's Eighth Symphony. The same work opens the 1995 Centenary Season*

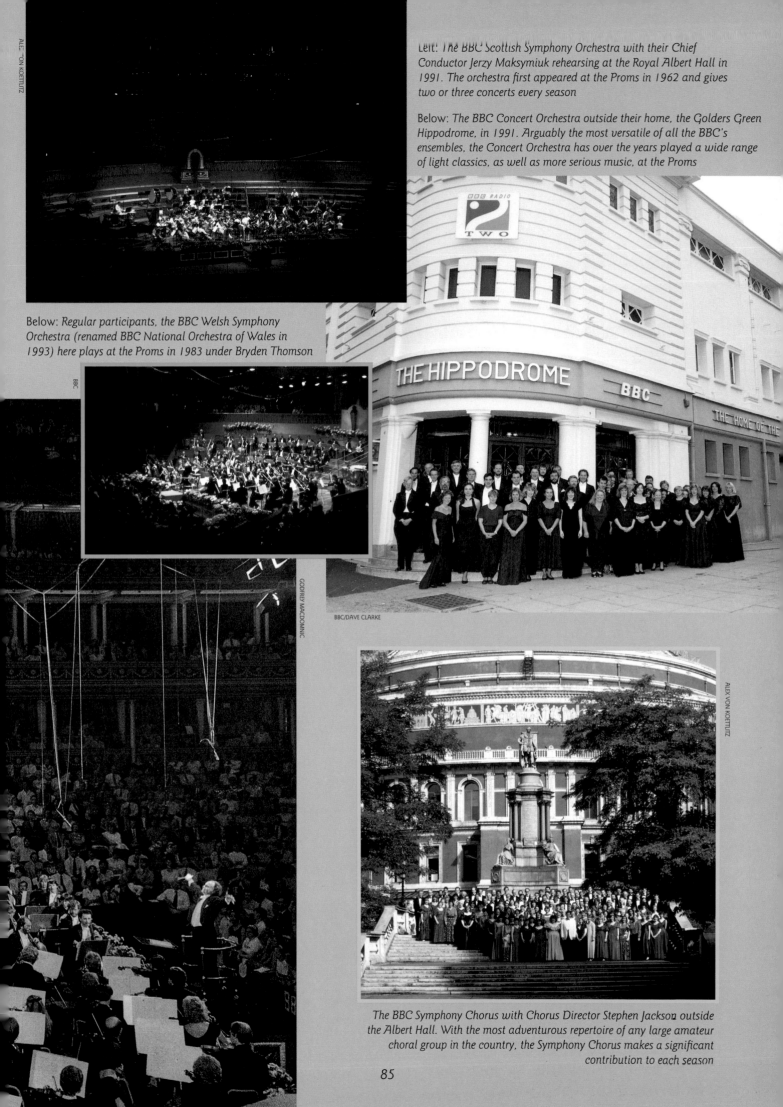

Left: The BBC Scottish Symphony Orchestra with their Chief Conductor Jerzy Maksymiuk rehearsing at the Royal Albert Hall in 1991. The orchestra first appeared at the Proms in 1962 and gives two or three concerts every season

Below: The BBC Concert Orchestra outside their home, the Golders Green Hippodrome, in 1991. Arguably the most versatile of all the BBC's ensembles, the Concert Orchestra has over the years played a wide range of light classics, as well as more serious music, at the Proms

Below: Regular participants, the BBC Welsh Symphony Orchestra (renamed BBC National Orchestra of Wales in 1993) here plays at the Proms in 1983 under Bryden Thomson

The BBC Symphony Chorus with Chorus Director Stephen Jackson outside the Albert Hall. With the most adventurous repertoire of any large amateur choral group in the country, the Symphony Chorus makes a significant contribution to each season

85

Below: *Though seriously ill, Sir John Pritchard was determined to conduct the Last Night of the 1989 Proms. His wit and strength of character were never better displayed than in his Last Night speech, a moment from which is captured here*

Above: *An exuberant Andrew Davis conducts the Verdi Requiem with the BBC SO on the First Night of the 1978 season. His soloists are Sylvia Sass, Alfreda Hodgson, Stuart Burrows and Gwynne Howell*

Below: Sir Colin Davis, Chief Conductor of the BBC SO between 1967 and 1971, and thereafter Chief Guest Conductor until 1976. His first Prom appearance was in the 1960 season and he has conducted over four hundred works in all

William Glock in bringing the finest of contemporary music to the Proms. His first appearance in 1965 included a performance of his own *Le Soleil des eaux*, and his final concert as Chief Conductor of the BBC SO, on 20 July 1975, featured his *Pli selon pli*. Rudolf Kempe, who followed Boulez, was an experienced Proms conductor, but died before being able to take the orchestra through the 1976 season. Gennady Rozhdestvensky (1978–81) was particularly notable for introducing a great deal of music from Russia and Eastern Europe, while Sir John Pritchard (1982–9), long associated with Glyndebourne, will always be remembered for his performances of Mozart. The orchestra's present Chief Conductor, Andrew Davis, made his Prom debut in 1971 and was entrusted with the First Night in both 1977 and 1978. He opened the 1990 season with a performance of Mahler's Second Symphony dedicated to the memory of John Pritchard, and has continued to give superb performances of music in the widest range of styles.

Andrew Davis and John Drummond outside the Albert Hall before the 1992 Press Conference

The BBC Singers in 1994, their seventieth season. This world-renowned choir appears regularly at the Proms, often performing the most challenging repertoire

Pierre Boulez conducts a performance of the Schumann Piano Concerto with the BBC SO in 1973. The soloist is Michael Roll, who has played on fourteen occasions

IN THE QUEEN'S HALL, W.I

SOLE LESSEES · MESSRS. CHAPPELL & CO., LTD.

Sir Colin Davis galvanising his players

oncerts

TED BY

Sir HENRY J. WOOD

SATURDAY, 6 AUGUST TO SATURDAY, I OCTOBER, 1938
AT 8 P.M.

Left: Seiji Ozawa conducts the Saito Kinen Orchestra in a performance of Brahms's First Symphony during the 1990 Proms

There is no one single ingredient that explains the success of the Proms. Looking back over a century, we can see that many different factors have contributed to their establishment, development and continuing excellence.

At the beginning, the most indispensable factor was perhaps the dedication and persistence of Henry Wood, who for nearly fifty years devoted himself to his favourite enterprise with courage, imagination and sheer hard work. As a result of these personal qualities, Wood was able to build up a uniquely close relationship between performers and audience which survived his death and continues as a feature of the Proms today. When it came to planning, Wood was severely practical about what was possible, but was never either patronising (giving the audience what they ought to like, whether they did or didn't) or ingratiating (rating the box office higher than musical experience). Today's planners are still keenly aware of the audience's close involvement in the music.

Ida Haendel playing Saint-Saëns's Third Violin Concerto on the Last Night of the 1989 Proms

Wood's encouragement of young artists was responsible for the launch of many a distinguished musical career, and this same faith in the future still contributes to the vitality of the Proms. Many young artists owe their first big chance to a Prom appearance. For some, it has been the beginning of a very long relationship with their audiences. The Prom career of Myra Hess lasted fifty-three years, and that of Ida Haendel (still going strong) approaches fifty-seven years. Sidonie Goossens, harpist of the BBC SO in 1930, made her final Prom appearance sixty-one years later in 1991. As for the audience, many of them owe a great part of their musical education to the Proms, and there must be many who have clocked up over half a century's attendance.

Tradition can be positive, but it can also be dangerous. In its worst sense, 'tradition' is simply a

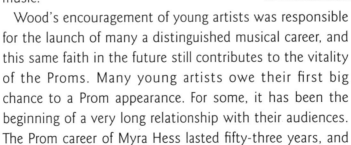

Dame Moura Lympany playing Rakhmaninov's Second Piano Concerto with the BBC SO under Vernon Handley in 1994

Every year during the Last Night of the Proms the bust of Sir Henry Wood, which has presided over the season, is crowned with a laurel wreath by two Promenaders

Left: *Riccardo Muti conducts the Philadelphia Orchestra in a performance of Schumann's Fourth Symphony, September 1982*

Günter Wand rehearses the BBC SO for a performance of Bruckner's Fifth Symphony on 4 September 1986. The concert was dedicated to the memory of Hans Keller

Peter Eötvös rehearses Debussy's Ibéria with the BBC SO in August 1984

Simon Rattle rehearses the City of Birmingham Symphony Orchestra for their Prom appearances in 1987. Sir Simon has appeared on thirty-three occasions since 1976

Below: *Pianist Radu Lupu (right) and conductor Riccardo Chailly compare notes at a rehearsal of Mozart's Piano Concerto K459 in September 1988*

A rehearsal of Walton's Violin Concerto in 1983. Sir John Pritchard conducts the BBC SO with soloist Iona Brown

Left: *In preparation for a performance of Mozart's Concerto K466 in August 1994. Later that season, Emanuel Ax also played the Schoenberg Concerto*

Below: *Mstislav Rostropovich conducts the European Community Youth Orchestra (now the European Union Youth Orchestra) in a performance of Prokofiev's Third Piano Concerto in August 1992. The pianist was Martha Argerich, whose only previous Prom appearance was in the same work in 1966*

ALEX VON KOETTLITZ

MALCOLM CROWTHERS

Above: *Yo-Yo Ma rehearses Strauss's Don Quixote in August 1982. Sir John Pritchard conducted the BBC SO. Yo-Yo Ma made his Prom debut in 1978 and has since appeared in six seasons*

ALEX VON KOETTLITZ

Above: *The baritone Benjamin Luxon and Andrew Davis before the Last Night of the 1988 season. As well as* Rule, Britannia!, *Luxon sang* Drake's Drum *by Stanford. The popular baritone has appeared on twenty-three occasions, including three Last Nights*

Russian pianist Tatyana Nikolaeva made an unforgettable impression with her two appearances on the last two nights of the 1992 season. She played a concerto by Bach and Shostakovich's Second

Right: Sir Peter Maxwell Davies directs tenor Neil Mackie in a rehearsal of his Into the Labyrinth *in 1984, one of twenty-five performances of his works since 1962. Most recently his Fifth Symphony received its world premiere in the 1994 season*

One less successful experiment was an evening in which the audience was invited to choose between three new works, by Don Banks, Thea Musgrave, and John Tavener, as to which of them they would like to hear again in the second half of the concert. It was not a very fruitful experiment, for the great majority of listeners voted for the most immediately attractive piece: John Tavener's In Alium. Bernard Levin, usually a warm ally of the new Proms, condemned the whole evening as an example of 'cheap huckstering', but it was in any case an idea to which we had no intention of returning.

William Glock, Notes in Advance (1991)

Witold Lutoslawski rehearsing the BBC SO for the UK premiere of his Symphony No. 4 at the 1993 Proms. Two years earlier, he had conducted the world premiere of his Chantefleurs et Chantefables

Evelyn Glennie demonstrates an aspect of percussion technique to composer James MacMillan before the world premiere of MacMillan's Veni, Veni, Emmanuel in 1992. In 1989 Glennie had been the first percussionist to be granted an entire Prom to herself

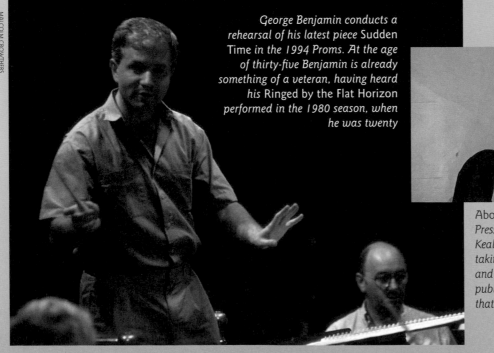

George Benjamin conducts a rehearsal of his latest piece Sudden Time in the 1994 Proms. At the age of thirty-five Benjamin is already something of a veteran, having heard his Ringed by the Flat Horizon performed in the 1980 season, when he was twenty

Above: Minna Keal with Oliver Knussen at the 1989 Press Conference. After early success in the 1920s, Keal relinquished composition for many years before taking it up once again as a pupil of Justin Connolly and then Knussen. He conducted the first complete public performance of her Symphony on 4 September that year

Elena Firsova, whose choral work Augury, commissioned by the BBC, received its world premiere in the 1992 season under Andrew Davis

comforting word for the repetition of old habits and formulae which have become lifeless. If the Proms have ever come close to this danger (and some people would say that it was a real danger by the end of the 1950s), they have been revitalised by the positive side of their tradition – an essential strength that can accommodate all sorts of changes without compromising their basic nature. This positive sense of tradition has given a momentum to the Proms, and ensured their continuation through situations that might easily have brought them to an end. Robert Newman's bankruptcy in 1904 and his death in 1926 threatened their existence, and so did two world wars. The fact that the Proms didn't come to grief was largely due to the fact that so many people insisted that they could not. The very size of the undertaking, as well as its venerable age, now guarantees its continuing momentum.

Vernon Handley conducts the Last Night of the 1985 season. In the far right of the front row of Promenaders stands a fourteen-year-old called Thomas Adès, whose own music would be heard at the Proms in ten years time

A further strength of the Proms is that they have risen to a level of excellence without ever running the danger of becoming exclusive. Money has often been a problem, and will probably continue to be so; but unlike certain other summer music festivals (let them remain nameless), the Proms do not draw their audiences from a wealthy or fashionable élite. They have always been inexpensive and truly popular.

No-one can doubt the continuing importance of the Proms as they set out on their second hundred years. One indication of their vitality is the level of public debate which they can stimulate. They are the country's most discussed musical enterprise. Planning and repertory are under constant discussion, both internally within the BBC and externally, in the press and in all circles which care about music. There is continuing debate about who should have ultimate responsibility for planning, and about whether

Berthold Goldschmidt appeared at the Proms in 1964 conducting the premiere of Deryck Cooke's performing version of Mahler's Tenth Symphony. This refugee from Nazi Germany had made England his home, though it was many years before his own music received its due in his adopted country. Simon Rattle conducted the London premiere of his Ciaconna sinfonica, composed in the mid-1930s, in 1993, when Goldschmidt was ninety years old

Composer Thea Musgrave with husband Peter Mark, who gave the world premiere of her Viola Concerto in 1973. Musgrave has had several Prom commissions over the years. The Centenary Season will include excerpts from her latest opera, Simón Bolívar

ROYAL ALBERT HALL/CHRIS CHRISTODOULOU

The BBC SO's percussion section demonstrate their versatility with a steam effect in the Waltz from Richard Rodney Bennett's Murder on the Orient Express, *Last Night, 1993*

BBC

Virtuoso pianolist Rex Lawson, with assistants Denis Hall and Peter Davis, check that their instrument is ready for Percy Grainger's return to the Proms in 1988

the necessary safe-guards exist to counter the dangers of personal prejudice. There is the perennial question of the ideal mixture of old and new music, young or established artists, British and foreign, the familiar and un-familiar. Choices are always difficult, for musical time is not unlimited: the 120-or-so hours of music which might be performed during a Prom season require careful balancing, since the inclusion of one item inevitably means the exclusion of something else.

The Proms have evolved over a century to become a uniquely rich festival, not just in the musical life of Britain, but in the whole world. The variety and quantity of music performed, the high standards of performance and the huge numbers of listeners cannot be matched by any other musical enterprise. Whatever changes occur in the future, the continued success of the Proms will be guaranteed if they follow the simple principle which inspired their beginnings in 1895 – to make the best music available to as wide an audience as possible.

BBC

Andrew Davis assists Percy Grainger from the stage at the end of their historic collaboration

BBC/ALEX VON KOETTLITZ

Left: John Tavener's The Apocalypse, *commissioned for the 1994 season, is one of the small number of pieces conceived especially for the unique space of the Royal Albert Hall. Here the composer is seen with treble soloist David Nickless*

Advertising the Proms in 1994

BBC/ALEX VON KOETTLITZ

ALEX VON KOETTLITZ

Left: Controller, Radio 3, and Proms Director designate Nicholas Kenyon (left) talks to presenter James Naughtie at the 1994 Press Conference

ALEX VON KOETTLITZ

John Drummond addresses BBC staff and representatives of the media at the 1994 Press Conference held on the stage of the Royal Albert Hall (and bottom left)

ALEX VON KOETTLITZ

ALEX VON KOETTLITZ

John Tavener (left) addresses Sir Harrison Birtwistle (right). Martin Cotton, the then Chief Producer of the BBC SO, listens attentively